Praise for *Higher and Hig*

'Please let Jost know that in my opinion he is one of the best speakers I have ever heard . . . I see Jost's work reaching much further than recovery from drug addiction. His description and understanding of the physical, emotional, mental and spiritual affects of organ dysfunction are fascinating and can only come from personal experience and an enormous amount of caring, dedicated and deeply intelligent healing practice. His exceptional ability to teach and write is destined to take all kinds of therapies to a higher level in one huge leap forward . . . the book is a masterpiece, a true reference book which has a place on every therapist's bookshelf.' —Jessica Read, Dr of Chiropractic and Holistic Healer

'Hey, Jost, your honesty is fantastic. Have drawn so much inspiration from your story.'—Pete

'Thank you for your site—you speak my language. I am starting the process of giving up dope after nearly 20 years of daily smoking.'—Karen

'I'm just writing to let you know how much I enjoyed your book . . . I keep reading out bits of your book to my mum because she's always asking me why people my age enjoy drugs so much. Some of your case studies could have been some of my own mates . . . I actually really felt sometimes like you were talking right to me! It's so good to know that you're not alone with these issues.'—Tara

Author biography

Jost Sauer is an acupuncturist, therapist and a one-time speed-addict, smuggler and deserter. Born in 1958 in Germany, Jost undertook studies in Social Pedagogics before arriving in Australia in 1981. After many years working in the field of youth drug and alcohol counselling, he completed a Bachelor of Health Science in Acupuncture, an Associate Diploma in Oriental Massage and certification in Sports Injury Management, Structural Balancing and Deep Tissue Massage. He has also studied Rolfing, Reiki and Body Harmony. Jost has been a practising therapist since 1991 and lectured in Traditional Chinese Medicine for a decade in Brisbane. In addition to his academic qualifications, his work is based on 20 years of spiritual practice. He is committed to health and healing on every level and has been undertaking a two-hour daily regime of exercise, chi-gung and meditation since 1985. He regularly presents meditation workshops and public seminars and his current area of research is the impact of recreational drug use on the body, mind and spirit.

For further information go to: www.jostsauer.com

HIGHER AND HIGHER

from drugs and destruction to health and happiness

Jost Sauer

ALLEN&UNWIN

This edition published by Allen & Unwin in 2006
First published in 2005 by Kijo Publications

Allen & Unwin
83 Alexander Street
Crows Nest NSW 2065
Australia
Phone: (61 2) 8425 0100
Fax: (61 2) 9906 2218
Email: info@allenandunwin.com
Web: www.allenandunwin.com

National Library of Australia
Cataloguing-in-Publication entry:

Sauer, Jost.
Higher and higher : from drugs and destruction to health
and happiness.

Bibliography.
    ISBN 978 1 74114 988 3.

    ISBN 1 74114 988 6.

    1. Sauer, Jost. 2. Drug abuse – Australia – Biography. 3.
    Drugs of abuse. 4. Medicine, Chinese. I. Title.

362.293092

Set in 11 on 14 pt Garamond Book by Midland Typesetters, Australia
Printed in Australia by McPherson's Printing Group

10 9 8 7 6 5 4 3 2 1

for Kirsten

Table of contents

Acknowledgements

I would like to thank all those people who contributed so much to the development of this book through their research, feedback, lively discussions, proofreading and editing. Foremost among them are the following:

My wife Kirsten, Kylie Fitzpatrick, Helena Bond, David Gidley, Dr Warren Stanton, Charlie Hogan, Holly Arden, Conan, Leon and Saul Fitzpatrick, Morgan Daly, Christoffer Forster, Geoff England, Simon Treselyan and all my students and patients over the years from whom I have learned so much.

I am especially grateful to the spiritual luminaries who have shared their knowledge in person or through their writings. Especially Bhai Sahib Kirpal Singh Ji Gill, who guided my research both theoretically and experientially.

Introduction

The 'war on drugs' has been lost. Illicit drugs are now one of the biggest businesses in the world. Although manufacturers and dealers have never spent a cent on advertising or promotion—in fact vast sums of money have been spent trying to prevent people from using their product—hundreds of millions of people take drugs, users are becoming younger and younger, and new drug markets keep 'opening up'. The United Nations Office on Drugs and Crime (UNODC) reports that in 2002, across all drug categories, nearly 26 billion 'unit equivalents'—a dose enough to give a high—were seized. At least ten times this probably remained in circulation: that's 260 billion highs.

The UNODC and many other drug authorities have now come to the understanding that, like any other business, drug markets are driven by demand and that giving demand as much attention as supply is a key strategy in dealing with the problem. However, neither the anti-drug campaigns nor the threat of criminal records or jail terms have affected market demand. This is because drugs make you feel good, and wanting to feel good is a pre-programmed human goal. I believe that we are spiritual beings driven to progress in life, to seek emotional mastery, spiritual fulfilment and unification of body, mind and spirit: in other words to feel good. Drugs appear to deliver this instantly; it's no wonder they are so popular.

If the desire to feel good is inherent in being human, then the only way to reduce the demand for drugs is to present a better product: a better way to feel good. According to my research, drugs generate those 'good' feelings by activating mechanisms that we already have within us, mechanisms that can be activated without drugs. It takes longer than popping a pill or puffing on a joint but it is worth it because, as I discovered myself, all drugs, even that 'harmless' one, marijuana, disrupt the delicate balances of the Human Energy Field and are spiritually, physically and emotionally depleting. They eventually deliver a smorgasbord of 'bad' feelings including frustration, cynicism, emptiness and depression: the very opposite to what was intended.

I believe that a lack of understanding of the full effects of drug use is also a contributing factor in their widespread use. This lack is due in part to the 'reductive' nature of Western medicine, its division between mind and body and its exclusion of the 'spiritual'. Western medicine also presents an implied sub-text that if you are not feeling good taking drugs 'fixes' things. In this book I use an analytical model based on my training in Traditional Chinese Medicine (TCM), Energy medicine, Body–Mind therapies and my research into spiritual practices, to explain the full physical, spiritual and emotional implications of drug use. Anyone who has used or is using drugs will appreciate the accessible and non-judgmental way the ideas are presented, interweaving a narrative documenting my own history of drug use and recovery with professional case studies and sociological, statistical and historical information. This analysis will also be of great interest to members of that ever-decreasing non-drug using sector of the population, as it offers an insight into the *desire* for drugs, as well as their effects on the total person.

If drugs are one of the biggest businesses in the world but drug use of any sort is going to affect you adversely, it stands to reason that drug recovery is going to become increasingly important and emphasis needs to shift to education and repair. In *Higher and Higher* I offer a unique body–mind–spirit workout that allows readers to discover just how good you can feel via a healthy and balanced lifestyle that unfolds in harmony with universal laws. It also presents a guide to integrating and making sense of past drug experiences and to reclaiming the exciting and exhilarating states that drugs once offered.

The text focuses on the use of commonly available illicit drugs. As post-drug depression is a rising concern, some coverage is also given to the selective serotonin reuptake inhibitors (SSRIs) which are currently amongst the best selling drugs in the world. The body makes no distinction between legal or illegal mood- and mind-altering drugs and many SSRIs can create similar side effects to speed or ecstasy. In addition, depletion from lifestyle choices can cause symptoms similar to drug use that every reader will recognise, and some common factors are analysed. Thus the information contained is equally applicable to non-drug users. Repair and recovery processes are the same, so *Higher and Higher* shows everyone a path to the ultimate high.

In addition, *Higher and Higher* offers an introduction to Traditional Chinese Medicine, a discipline which I believe is well placed to address pathologies and imbalances arising from 21st century Western lifestyles. The book is based primarily on the research and pathology of Traditional Chinese Medicine and anecdotal and experiential evidence of the effects of common illicit drugs and SSRIs, rather than a comprehensive, scientific analysis of all available drugs.

The terminology used follows the conventions often used in the translations of Traditional Chinese Medicine to English. Capitals are used for terms used in a sense specific to Traditional Chinese Medicine such as Chi, Liver, Spleen, Blood and so on.

CHAPTER ONE

Sex and drugs and freeflow

FOLK FESTIVAL, SUMMER 1977

The summer morning air was scented with sandalwood, marijuana and hashish. I walked barefoot through the tents and groups of colourfully dressed hippies, until I reached the clearing in the trees that formed a natural amphitheatre. My friends, Dietrich and Karl, were sitting on the grass near the stage and I wandered over to join them. A folk band was playing, setting the mood for another day of music, dancing and euphoria. Dietrich offered me a half-smoked joint. He had such a big smile on his face that it was obviously not his first smoke for the day. Karl's face was painted in psychedelic colours and he too was grinning widely. I sat with them and we shared the rest of the joint. The amphitheatre was slowly filling up. Joan Baez was on stage next and a sense of anticipation was building.

I felt an arm around my shoulder and turned to see Stefan, my best friend. His brown eyes were dancing with excitement and he was holding up a small, engraved silver box. He opened the lid ceremoniously to reveal four tiny red stars nestled in cotton wool; our first LSD experience was about to begin. Karl, Dietrich and I sat in a semi-circle around Stefan and watched intently as his long beringged fingers delicately lifted out the little stars. He handed us one each.

I placed mine carefully under my tongue. Almost instantly I felt a strange metallic sensation in my mouth which gradually spread throughout my body. I sat back, rolled a cigarette and enjoyed the nurturing atmosphere of the crowd and the music. Then I noticed a feeling of warmth in my stomach. It slowly intensified until it filled my consciousness. I had an irresistible urge to move and I began to sway. My hands became hyper-sensitive; just holding my cigarette was an amazing tactile experience. My head and neck felt like they were floating above my body.

I looked at Karl. The painted colours were now swirling around his face and through his long blond hair. His eyes met mine and we both burst into fits of laughter. Spontaneously we jumped up and hugged each other. The others rose to share in the euphoria and the rhythm of the music began to really move us. But the source didn't seem to be the stage anymore; it was coming from the ground, like a root. I could feel it creeping up my legs and spreading through my entire body, creating waves of ecstasy.

I stopped thinking and simply became the experience. I began to walk around. With every step I discovered new sensations. The grass under my feet was sharp but soft, cool but warm, and I could feel the breeze drifting through my hair, caressing my scalp. I lifted my arms; there was no resistance. It was as if they floated up. I was weightless—body, mind and spirit were united. I looked at the people around me and smiled at everyone. I started to dance and my heart sang out in sheer joy.

A group of trees at the edge of the clearing were slowly morphing into huge majestic animals. One tree in particular seemed to make contact with me. Transfixed by its powerful presence, I walked over to it. I had a strong urge to show respect and I bowed humbly and gently touched its surface. I looked back towards the stage; it was now surrounded by a bright, soft, purple light and the massive banks of speakers were a pulsating, luminous green. The sky was iridescent blue. Distance didn't seem to exist anymore. I could hear the conversations of people who were completely out of my sight but I knew that I could reach them instantly if I wanted to. Everyone was a part of me just as I was a part of them.

Then Joan Baez walked out onto the stage. She picked up her guitar and began to sing. The purity of her voice tore through the tissue of my heart and reverberated through every cell in my body. Time stopped still. I stood there completely immersed in a state of pure joy. Tears ran down my face as I realised just how beautiful the world could be.

That first acid trip was a beautiful spiritual experience. It satisfied the deepest desires of my soul. I thought I had reached the ultimate goal of human existence. I felt utterly complete. I was nineteen but I had never felt so alive, so real. It was as if a filter had been removed and all my senses could now function at optimum level. I could taste colour, see sound, hear people's thoughts. I was everything I could ever be, all at once and I wanted more of that. I spent the next decade chasing that state through drugs but I never again recaptured that perfect intoxicating mix of exhilaration, liberation and euphoria; the thrill of the realisation that the world was going to change and the anticipation of a life of limitless opportunity and wonder stretching ahead of me.

Instead, that magical, colourful hippie world collapsed and my dreams vanished with it. The drugs that I used to try to generate that state took me to the depths of despair and the brink of death. I lost my passion to change the world and was left with depression, emptiness and a sense of loss. It took me years of experiential and theoretical research into health, fitness and self-improvement to regain some excitement about life and to discover that what I had been searching for had been within me all the time.

By the time that I had recovered from my drug-induced destruction and become a therapist and lecturer in Traditional Chinese Medicine (TCM), the New Age movement had also emerged from the ashes of the hippie movement and our dream of creating a better world and acknowledging our spiritual nature had entered mainstream society. Twenty years after that first acid trip, I found myself back at colourful festivals but now I was showing people how to get high— how to recapture the euphoria, bliss and bonding that the drugs had shown so many of us—without the drugs.

BODY, MIND AND SPIRIT FESTIVAL

I ran up the stairs of the Convention Centre, squeezed past the queues of people in their bright summer clothes, and flashed my exhibitor's pass at the entry. Coloured lights, ambient music and exotic fragrances overwhelmed my senses as I stepped inside. The Body, Mind and Spirit festival was set up like a huge supermarket with aisle after aisle of display stands laden with products and information about how to be happy and healthy. It was early, but the place was teeming with people and it was hard going navigating through the narrow aisles.

Movement on the mezzanine level caught my eye and I glanced up. What looked like hundreds of people were filing out of the lecture theatre and coming down the stairs into the main hall. The first talk must have just finished. I would be up there next. Butterflies fluttered lightly in my stomach. I had been lecturing about energy freeflow in an academic environment for nearly a decade, but today would be the first time that I explained it to the general public.

I glanced at my watch. I still had about fifteen minutes before I was due to speak, so after checking in with the team of massage therapists working on my clinic's stand, I went off in search of a place to do some meditative exercises and centre myself. Eventually I found an empty area sectioned off from the surrounding stalls by large partitions. I ducked behind them. It was still noisy but at least I was out of sight of the crowd. I stood still and tried to regulate my breathing and sink into a deeper part of my mind.

This was just starting to take effect when a group of belly-dancers trooped in, chattering and laughing. I had obviously found a warm-up area for one of the performance stages. The dancers didn't seem concerned by my presence and started rehearsing their routine behind me. I tried not to let them distract me, closed my eyes and continued to focus my mind—breath by breath. I could feel my breath start to connect with my inner energy, or Chi, and the sounds around me began to fade. I used each inhalation to move Chi around in my body until it was circulating freely. I continued doing this for about ten minutes before opening my eyes.

Slowly my senses registered the material world again. The colourful sequinned costumes of the dancers flashed past me. I could smell incense and hear Indian sitar music in the background. I felt focused and grounded. I took a breath, nodded to the dancers, and headed off in the direction of the lecture hall. Calm and confident, I glided effortlessly through the crowds until my name and lecture topic came blasting through the public address system, shaking my equilibrium. But the meditation had done its job and, after a brief moment of stress, I managed to recapture my sense of centre.

As I reached the stairs to the mezzanine level, I realised that most of the people around me were heading in the same direction. I was surprised at the number; I had not thought that 'Sex and drugs and freeflow' would be such a crowd pleaser. Inside the lecture theatre most of the chairs were already filled. I walked over to the speaker's stand, turned the microphone on and set my papers out in front of me. I quickly flipped through my notes as the last few people trickled through the door. There was a quiet murmur in the audience. Fifteen seconds to go. I took a deep breath, made a conscious connection with my Chi again to ground myself, then the minute hand hit the hour and I started to speak. The background noise stopped instantly and three hundred eyes focused on me, watching my every move and analysing every word. I felt that they were seeking weakness. It was always a testing moment but my Chi was strong enough and I felt in control. I launched into the lecture.

SEX AND DRUGS AND FREEFLOW

'My topic today is "Sex and drugs and freeflow". I'll start with drugs. Illicit drugs are a multi-billion dollar, global business, probably one of the biggest industries in the world. Basically this is because they take away pain, they make you feel good, they make you happy. So I guess you could say that it is really the search for happiness that is one of the biggest industries in the world.

'Put up your hand if you want to feel happy.' Everyone in the room put their hands up and there were a few laughs.

'We all want to feel good, and we all want to be happy. But drugs can only deliver this in the short term so eventually we have to find other more sustainable ways of achieving this result. This is an area I have been investigating and, based on my background of personal drug use and my subsequent research into Traditional Chinese Medicine, Energy medicine, Body–Mind therapy and spirituality, I believe that drugs create feelings of bliss because they allow energy, or Chi, to move freely in the body. This is a state which I call 'freeflow' and it is this that we need to experience pure happiness. The moment of orgasm or the rush you get from snorting cocaine are both good examples of freeflow.'

The freeflow state

'The concept of freeflow is based on the idea that the body has an invisible energetic structure, generally referred to in Energy medicine as the Human Energy Field. Although this might sound New Age, this same idea forms the basis of Traditional Chinese Medicine, which has been around for five thousand years. Generally speaking, both streams of practice would suggest that you feel good when Chi, or inner energy, flows freely in the body, and bad when Chi is stagnant or not flowing freely. The objective of my work as a therapist—in which I draw upon many therapeutic disciplines—is to clear the blockages or obstructions so that Chi can flow freely and you can feel good again.'

I turned to the whiteboard behind me and used a black marker to draw an outline of a body. It looked like one of those chalk bodies drawn at the sites of accidents but it would have to do. I then used a red marker to draw lines throughout the body with dots at intervals along the lines. Now it looked like a human subway map.

'In Traditional Chinese Medicine, Chi flows within the body via pathways which are known in the West as the acupuncture meridians. These meridians have intersections and openings which are the acupuncture points. If you are in perfect health, the Chi flows along the meridians and at the acupuncture points it divides. It then flows outwards to nurture skin, tendons and muscles, which allows the body to move effortlessly. It also flows inwards to the organs establishing perfect organ function.' I chose a green marker and roughly drew the lungs, heart, liver, spleen and kidneys in the torso. It was not anatomically correct but the aim was to connect the organs to the red "subway map" of the meridians.

'As well as having a physiological function, each of your organs also has a spiritual and emotional function. So, in the state of freeflow, where the organs have abundant Chi and function perfectly, you feel great physically, spiritually and emotionally.' All eyes were fixed on the whiteboard trying to grasp this information. Given the venue, most of my audience would have heard of acupuncture points and maybe even the Human Energy Field, but the idea that the condition of your organs might directly affect or even create your emotional state would probably be new to them. I paused for a moment before turning back to the board and pointing at each of the organs in turn.

'My work fuses Traditional Chinese Medicine, Energy medicine and Body–Mind therapy, and it's this fusion, rather than a pure application of any one of these approaches, which applies to most of what I say from now on. In the state of freeflow the Lungs let you embrace change, let go of the past and look forward to the future. The Heart generates feelings of love, inspiration and joy. The Liver makes you feel that your life is progressing as it should be and this makes you happy. The Spleen makes you feel energetic and provides a balanced sense of self. In addition your thoughts will flow smoothly and you will be able to grasp complex concepts and ideas easily. The Kidneys make you feel young and full of zest. You will have plenty of will-power and feel "supported" in everything you do.

'This is freeflow, a blissfully happy state in which you love yourself, the world and everyone in it. You feel no pain, hold no grudges and only look forward. Life is full of promise. You sleep peacefully through the night and wake up full of energy and anticipation, eager to jump out of bed and get into another exciting and joyful day. Nothing and nobody affects your peace of mind.' I let my arm drop.

'Who feels like this all the time?' I paused and scanned the room, but no one raised a hand. They were reacting as I had hoped. I rephrased the question. 'Who would like to feel like this all the time?' Laughter erupted, some hands slowly rose, and eventually all hands were up, including mine.

'So why don't we feel like this? As you can see, we all have the mechanisms in place in our organs to make us feel fantastic all the time, so what is the problem?' I picked up the red marker and drew a large dot on top of one of the acupuncture points in the shoulder of my diagram man, before answering my own question. 'The problem is that if there is a blockage at an acupuncture point, only a small amount of Chi can squeeze through. This is like a traffic jam where six lanes of traffic turn into one and then only one car at a time can pass. As a result the organs do not get enough Chi to function effectively and your spiritual, emotional and physical wellbeing suffers.' I drew a table on the whiteboard showing examples of some positive and negative states and emotions associated with each of the organs I had drawn.

Organ	Positive aspect	Negative aspect
Lungs	Spontaneity	Sadness/grief
Heart	Joy/excitement	Depression/shock
Liver	Happiness	Frustration/anger
Spleen	Clarity of thought/vitality	Confusion/obsession
Kidneys	Strength/will-power	Weakness/fear

The non-freeflow state

I started the organ circuit again by pointing at the Lungs. 'Now, in the obstructed version in which the organs are not functioning properly, the Lungs make you feel constricted rather than spontaneous. You find it hard to accept change, detach from the past or embrace the future. You feel sadness or grief and have a sense of not being in control.

'The Heart is also deprived of Chi, so it generates feelings of depression and disillusionment, you experience anxiety or insomnia or both and feel like you are in a state of shock. You are in a non-love relationship with yourself, others and the world.

'Now the Liver makes you feel like you are driving with the handbrake permanently on, creating frustration, anger or resentment. As the Spleen can't function properly, you feel constantly tired. You wake up and don't want to get out of bed. When you do get up, you just can't get going. The whole day is a drag. Your body aches and feels heavy and your muscles are tight. Your posture is hunched. You don't ever feel really present. It takes a huge amount of effort to think and then even more of an effort to get your thoughts and your words across clearly. It is almost as if the muscles in your mouth don't have the energy to do the job of speaking, so you have no desire to communicate with anyone.'

I could see quite a few people responding with surprised looks or slight nods. What we call 'Spleen Chi deficiency' in TCM, or lack of Chi in the Spleen, was becoming a major health issue and, as many people in the audience probably had that condition, I decided to go into more detail about the associated symptoms.

'In the West most of us have no idea what the Spleen does, but Traditional Chinese Medicine sees its role as crucial: it is considered responsible for transforming foods into energy. However, due to factors such as our nutrient-poor diet of processed foods with high sugar and fat levels, this function is becoming seriously affected in many people. I believe Spleen Chi deficiency is now a serious health issue in Western society. It is a problematical condition too because if you become Spleen Chi deficient, you will have no appetite for healthy foods, which is what you need, but frequent cravings for sweet or high fat snacks, which make the condition worse.

'With weakened Spleen function, your ability to concentrate and focus will also decline. Your mind feels dull and sort of "detached" from your body. You sit in front of a computer or book and read the same sentence over and over again. As the Spleen is also responsible for transportation of thought, you can start to lose track of what you were saying in the middle of a sentence. If the person you are talking to is thrown by this, they may stare at you, waiting for you to finish what you were saying. If you can't pick up the thread it can start a cycle where you feel uneasy at social events. You know that something isn't quite right but it is too strange to talk about, so you ignore it hoping it will go away, but it won't. Eventually, you can end up trapped in your mind thinking things over obsessively and losing all objectivity. Then, in an attempt to seek some sort of relief or sense of movement, you may project your emotional anguish and confusion onto others in the form of accusation, anger or recrimination.' I paused to let the implications sink in, then pointed at the Kidneys.

'Weakened Kidney function can make you feel old and worn-out. You lack will-power, vitality and confidence and you are fearful about life. You also have the sense of being unsupported. Physically, your lower back hurts, your legs feel weak, your knees feel sore and the frequent need for urination makes everything even worse. Interest in sex declines and, if there is sexual activity, it is characterised in men by premature ejaculation or loss of erection in the middle of the act. In women there is a loss of libido. Quite simply, the spark of life is gone. Dark shadows under the eyes and pale skin are two signs of advanced Kidney Chi deficiency.' I paused, and a few people glanced around, obviously wondering if they could spot any symptoms of this in their neighbours.

'Who in this room can relate to any of these symptoms?' I asked. Instantly every hand was raised, including mine, and everyone laughed again. I had to raise my voice to overpower the noise—a good sign.

'So what can we do about it?' An expectant silence met this question.

I moved back to the whiteboard and pointed to the blocked acupuncture point. 'These obstructed acupuncture points are the problem because they stop the Chi flowing freely. So, if we want to feel good we need to get the body back to a state of freeflow, but the question is, how do we do this?' I looked around the room, making eye contact with as many people as possible.

Drugs and freeflow

'Fortunately, there is a method that will sort the problem out within minutes.' Now I really had their attention. All eyes were focused on me, waiting for this magical solution. 'A quick snort of some good quality cocaine would instantly make all these symptoms disappear and replace them with the thrilling and exhilarating experience of freeflow.' As I had hoped, a stunned silence met this remark. Most people stared at me in total disbelief. This was supposed to be a natural health lecture and I appeared to be enthusiastically advocating the use of illicit drugs to deal with health problems.

'This is because, like most stimulants, legal or illegal, cocaine forces an instant freeflow of Chi. As soon as the drug enters your system, Chi rushes along all the meridians. When it hits a blockage at an acupuncture point the drug acts like a bulldozer that pushes the traffic jam through the blocked intersection and forces the Chi to keep flowing. The pathway to the Lungs suddenly becomes free. As Lungs represent "the moment", you instantly feel what it is like to truly live in the moment. All the pain of old relationships, disputes and grudges is gone, along with heaviness, grief or sadness. You feel completely spontaneous. When abundant Chi floods the

Heart, shock, anxiety or depression are replaced by intense joy, excitement and love.'

I pointed to the Liver. 'When the Liver comes under the influence of the cocaine-induced freeflow, anger and frustration instantly disappear. Stress also vanishes. Time loses its suffocating presence and you feel perfectly in tune with life. The drug freeflow artificially enhances your Spleen function too. Thinking becomes clear and structured again and information can be absorbed and understood in seconds. Formulating and expressing your thoughts is effortless, so communicating and problem solving become pleasurable and you actively seek people to talk to.

'Abundant Chi in the Kidneys means that lack of confidence and fear are replaced by self-assurance and willpower. You feel like you've got "backbone" and "balls" and you have the energy to move or dance all night. Sexual energy reaches new heights too and you can make love for hours on end without the urge to climax.' I glanced around the room: in spite of their discomfort with the method I'd proposed, the desire for lots of Kidney Chi was written on everyone's faces.

'Cocaine definitely works, it delivers dramatic results. In a recent book about the drug the author describes the effects as follows: "the moment you shove it up your nose it races into your bloodstream, heads directly into the pleasure centre of your brain, kicks down the door, jams your Fun Throttle forwards into 'way too fast' and dumps the clutch" (Streatfeild 2001, p. x), and I can confirm that every word of this is true. So, why not use cocaine all day long and enjoy the pleasures of freeflowing Chi?' I paused, pretending to expect an answer, but there was only silence.

Drugs and Jing

'Unfortunately the freeflow a drug like cocaine generates is not naturally induced, so ultimately it comes at a high price. If you use the vocabulary of Traditional Chinese Medicine to explain the fantastic rush you get from snorting cocaine, it does not come from something in that white powder, it occurs because the cocaine draws upon an internal power, known as Jing. Jing is the fuel for all our physical, emotional and spiritual activities.

'Part of your Jing is given to you at birth. This is known as pre-natal Jing. The other part, the post-natal Jing, is derived from your food intake and managed by your lifestyle. Jing determines your basic constitutional strength and vitality. The more Jing you have the more you can enjoy life. Traditional Chinese Medicine, which is essentially a preventative medicine, aims to conserve, support and nurture your Jing.

'Drugs do the exact opposite. Each drug high draws upon your store of Jing, initiates premature ageing and moves you one step closer to death. Powerful stimulants like cocaine need massive amounts of Jing to create the impression of perfect organ function. As Jing depletes you are less able to enjoy life and need more cocaine to feel good. However, if you continue using the drug it inevitably becomes a cycle of more organ damage, more side effects and less pleasure. It is in situations like this that cocaine, or synthetic stimulants such as speed, can act as gateway drugs to heroin. After a period of heroin addiction, however, the Jing is so depleted that no drug can give you a high.

'From here the only options are to re-build your Jing and organ function, or choose death via what we used to call the "golden shot". At this stage the latter can be an appealing option because once your organ function has deteriorated so badly, you already feel "worse than death" anyway. Drugs such as cocaine, speed or ecstasy are extremely destructive to the Human Energy Field. Even though the highs they generate may feel beneficial in the short term, it is the state of the Human Energy Field that determines the health of the body, and drugs will create additional distortions or obstructions and make existing ones even worse.

'Drugs don't create positive change and drugs don't generate health or happiness. Blockages in the Energy Field are still present and active, you just aren't aware of them when you are high.'

I glanced around the room. By now the audience was clear that I wasn't advocating cocaine as a way to achieve health and happiness. The atmosphere had become serious. It was time to shake them up again.

Sex and freeflow

'So, if we can't take drugs because ultimately they make the situation worse, what other freeflow options do we have? What about sex? Having sex is a great way to feel good. This is because, like drugs, sexual activities also create a temporary freeflow of energy. Fortunately, there is the difference that, as long as it is healthy sex, it will not have any negative effects on the Human Energy Field—and it is usually legal.'

I paused for a moment and slowly looked around the room. 'I want everyone to imagine themselves twenty seconds before orgasm.' Most people laughed, and there were a few smiles as they tried to oblige while not looking at each other.

'When you are that close to orgasm your Energy Field is completely under the influence of the sexual stimulus,

20

therefore Chi flows freely. So, like on a drug, blockages are bypassed and Chi circulates in the internal organ system. Your breathing becomes deep and effortless and the Lungs manifest spontaneity. You don't lie there thinking about the past or the future. You don't think, "Should I lift this leg now, or bend this elbow?", you are fully in the present and everything happens naturally.

'The Heart makes you feel inspired and in love and you use verbal, aural and tactile means to express this love. Sensations of intense joy wash over you. The Spleen generates clarity. You know just who you are and what you want. The Liver fully immerses you in the experience of action, and stress, anger and frustration don't exist. As orgasm approaches, the Kidneys make even more energy available, tiredness and fatigue vanish and the experience intensifies almost unbearably. Then you orgasm and nothing else matters.' A wave of laughter washed through the room.

'Sex does make the Chi flow, and it can clear minor obstructions making you feel temporarily uplifted and relaxed. Unfortunately though, an orgasm doesn't last all day and having sex cannot change the circumstances that created the blockages in the first place. For example, imagine yourself rushing to work, late for an important meeting. Every traffic light turns red just as you approach it. You have no sense of movement, the Chi in the Liver begins to stagnate and you feel frustrated and angry. A quick orgasm could move the Chi but as a stress management technique it is not very reliable because eventually the body will boycott it to avoid energy depletion. Orgasm draws upon the Jing, particularly in men, so too much sex will eventually deplete the body. Not only that, but there are other obvious problems associated with having sex in peak-hour traffic.'

Therapy and freeflow

'So we have to find other ways of dealing with these energetic obstructions and getting the Chi to flow freely again.
This is where a program of therapy, spiritual practice, exercise and nutritional supplements comes into the picture. It
doesn't sound as much fun as sex and drugs, but in the long
term such a program can create constant freeflow and it
doesn't get much better than that.'

I pointed at the blocked acupuncture point again.
'Although this blockage is not visible, in therapeutic terms
we treat it as a crystalline structure. Energy medicine is based
on an understanding that these crystalline blockages have
similar organic properties, or behave in a similar way, to the
crystals used in many commercial applications. The key
similarities are that they are capable of storing energy and
they are also "piezo-electric" which means that when pressure is applied to them this stored energy can emanate
(Oschman 2000, p. 52). So, if we put these crystals under
pressure, using acupuncture, massage or other techniques,
the blockages will reduce in size and the Chi can flow again.

'This allows increased amounts of Chi to move along the
meridians, nourishing the skin, and lubricating the tendons
and muscles. At the same time the Chi flows inwards and
begins correcting organ imbalances. After a time, pain and negative emotions, which were a result of blockages and impaired
organ function, are gradually replaced with the harmonious
feelings of freeflow. As no corruptive methods such as drugs
were used to bypass the blockage, there are no side effects and
you are on the path of constant improvement.'

A young woman with spiky red hair raised her hand. 'You
have made the healing process sound quite mechanical, with

the piezo-electric effect and so on, as if any of us could do some training, apply pressure to the correct spot, prescribe supplements and achieve these results, but there are many people here at the festival who present themselves as natural healers, do you think there is such a thing?'

She had highlighted one of the difficulties of the holistic health movement, the fact that under the one New Age umbrella there were all kinds of people from crystal-dangling hobbyists to professional therapists who had—through years of training and discipline—mastered a technique that could help people change on a much more profound level. Both ends of the spectrum were probably represented in my audience. I phrased my answer carefully.

'Medical research into magnetobiology, the study of the effects of magnetic fields on living systems, has established that magnetic fields can be used to accelerate healing in tissues as long as forty years after the original injury occurred. It has also been discovered that the hands of some trained Energy therapists can emit biomagnetic fields of a similar frequency to those generated by the devices used by the medical institutions (Oschman 2000, p. 78). I think that there are some people who have a natural talent in this area and are attracted to the healing professions but in my opinion, the degree to which they can be effective is directly connected to the amount of effort they invest in mastering and understanding their own Chi. The stronger their own Chi is, the more powerful their work will be because the more effective they will be at reducing blockages in the Energy Fields of their patients.'

She looked at me quizzically and then said, 'But if you use your own Chi to move the blocked energy of the patient, isn't there a danger that whatever has caused their blockage could then affect you?' She must have studied or at least read about Energy medicine because she was nailing the major challenges of the job.

'The answer to your question would have to be—yes. Whatever is stored in the patient's Energy Field can, in certain circumstances, move to the therapist's Energy Field. So, the more effective and intense the treatment, the more stress can be placed on the organs of the therapist. For example, the Spleen is often affected as it is the organ for digesting emotionality. I believe that Energy therapists need to undergo many years of Chi-training in order to understand how to modulate the patient's Energy Field without depleting their own energy and affecting their own organs. This is really challenging though, and most graduates from natural medicine courses in the West are not aware of such potential side effects, and not adequately trained in how to deal with them. The result is a high burn-out rate.'

She then asked me how I personally avoided burn-out.

'After I finish working on a patient I take at least ten minutes to rebalance myself,' I responded. 'I also spend a lot of time each day building my Chi: two hours each morning of stretching, meditation, endurance exercise and Tai-chi. This is followed by a breakfast of porridge made from organic oats which I have soaked overnight. Lunch is Asian-style meals of rice, vegetables and organic lamb or beef.' I could see a small shock wave move through the audience when I mentioned eating meat. It was a definite no-no in New Age circles.

'I never have fat or protein in the evening, so for dinner I usually eat unbuttered toast made from good quality bread. In addition, I have regular weekly Bodywork treatments and I take herbs and nutritional supplements on a regular basis. I never deviate from this routine during the week, and if I do

I can instantly feel the negative effects. Even one biscuit for morning tea would severely affect my Chi, as the sugar has immediate detrimental effects on the Spleen.' The audience looked downcast at this grim picture of my lifestyle.

'I know it doesn't sound like much fun, but I do have a couple of light beers each night. If I feel like "entertainment food", such as cakes or biscuits, I eat it on weekends or holidays, when it is not going to affect my energy for work. In my opinion health is a science and if you follow a structured health plan your life will improve dramatically.'

A man at the back of the room raised his hand and asked why I took supplements when I obviously had such a healthy diet.

'The existence of the Human Energy Field and freeflow indicates that all we need for health and happiness is already within us and probably always has been. However, new lifestyle factors such as pollution, drugs and highly-processed food stripped of nutrient value, constantly deplete our energy. I don't believe that we can counter all these negative elements anymore without help. Preventative medicine is the way of the future and a key element of preventative medicine and anti-ageing is supplementation. If you boost your whole system with the correct supplements it encourages freeflow by assisting in re-balancing the organs and it also assists in breaking down blockages. However, you have to use an effective product and it needs to be managed by a professional.

'Many people self-prescribe vitamins. In most cases this is ineffective and a waste of money or even dangerous, as incorrect supplementation can disturb the equilibrium of the body and do more damage than good. There are many things that you can do of your own accord to help to de-obstruct your Energy Field and generate freeflow. Things like improving your diet, changing your mental attitude and taking up exercise, yoga or Tai-chi, but with all of these and with supplements in particular, I would recommend professional advice to make it as effective as possible.'

FREEFLOW FEST

The hall was packed with people and I could barely move through the aisles. It suddenly occurred to me that everyone in the festival was either offering or searching for ways of achieving happiness or freeflow. It was a fundamental need in life. I had been too busy running my stand to look around the festival properly, so I decided to take a desperately needed coffee break and see what was on offer. I set off through the hall in the general direction of the café.

Herbal highs

Funnily enough, given my lecture topic, the first thing to catch my attention was a stall selling herb combinations that claimed to get you legally high. It had a large crowd in front of it, all jostling to see the goods for sale. The vendor was wearing a patchwork harlequin outfit and an oversized top hat with a multi-coloured furry rainbow glued onto it. He reminded me of someone I had seen at a hippie festival in Germany. Both men were tall and skinny and wore similar outfits but the German used his hat as a store for the LSD that he distributed to the crowd! I was pretty sure I wouldn't be finding that here today but I edged in closer to have a look.

A wide variety of herb mixtures, with names like ecstasy, dope and bliss, packed in small plastic bags ready for consumption were neatly displayed on the counter. Reggae music throbbed in the background. I could almost imagine that I was back in Amsterdam at one of the famed cafés, examining a range of hashish packed in plastic bags. But this was Australia and the crowd was full of people seeking natural ways of achieving health and happiness.

The herb-vendor looked happy, but it was probably because of the large number of people purchasing his goods rather than as a result of taking his own products. I grabbed one of his leaflets which claimed that these herbs were a harmless and legal way to get high. I considered it a bit misleading. Herbal medicine is extremely complex. Each herb targets a specific organ function and should be professionally administered in response to presenting symptoms. If a herb is self-administered over a long period of time for recreational purposes, instead of creating organ balance it can actually generate imbalances. For example, tonifying and stimulating herbs like ginseng, guarana and others frequently used in these mixtures or even in the new range of 'energy soft-drinks', can be 'hot' in nature. Excessive intake of them can allow heat to accumulate in the body and a heat pathology can develop.

Many of my students thought that such legal herbal mixtures were harmless and took them regularly. They couldn't imagine that herbs could have side effects. One student in particular, who was studying and working full time, had been taking potent ginseng formulas to try and increase her energy. She had found herself becoming more and more aggressive and wound-up. Walking quickly through the city one day she found herself caught behind a group of elderly people crossing a road, and she felt like screaming at them to move. She was horrified at her reaction and went to see a Chinese herbalist. It turned out that her tiredness was caused by an energetic imbalance and self-administering ginseng was the opposite of what was needed. Like supplements, herbs should be prescribed by a professional and be used to build Yin and Yang in balance. This creates the basis for healthy and long-lasting freeflow.

Charismatic religion

I put the brochure back on the table and drifted with the crowd to another stand belonging to some sort of spiritual organisation. There was none of the clutter and colour of the herb stand here. This stall was empty except for a single chair in the middle of the space. Half a dozen well-dressed men were standing around the perimeter handing out leaflets and inviting people in. Apparently the chair was used for initiating volunteers into a charismatic movement and setting them on the road to salvation. Again, the underlying appeal of charismatic movements is the freeflow states they can generate.

I picked up a flyer to see which particular school of thought the stand belonged to. A clean-shaven man in a suit immediately came up to me and offered me the chair. I guessed he was in his early thirties. As he came closer I noticed that his ears had rows of pierced holes but no earrings. Despite his carefully constructed 'presentable appearance' his past had obviously been quite different. I was interested in how he had ended up there and started to chat to him to find out about it, but our conversation was quickly cut off by one of his equally friendly colleagues, with an even bigger smile, who came over to steer the conversation firmly in the direction of spirituality. Unfortunately I was more interested in his past so I thanked him and then moved on with the flow of the crowd.

Drums and crystals and chakras

The sound of drums led me on, and I followed the noise to a large stand where Hawaiian Bodyworkers in bright floral shirts and sarongs were moving rhythmically around several massage tables. Their almost hypnotic, dance-like movements and the wild throbbing of the drums had drawn a large crowd. As one of their tables became free, I was tempted to have a massage, but the thought of getting back into my clothes after what was essentially an oil bath counteracted my desire for such a smooth and oozy, but highly rewarding, freeflow experience.

I let myself get carried on by the crowd and stopped next at an impressive looking crystal-healing stand. Thousands of crystals, suspended from the ceiling, were spinning slowly, throwing rainbows of coloured light across the floor. Each crystal promised all sorts of physical, emotional or spiritual assistance. The stall-holder was thin with a slightly withdrawn face and long, wispy, blond hair. He was dressed in a dark blue robe and had a massive crystal pendant hanging around his neck. His stand emanated a strong sense of serenity and commitment.

Despite the fact that the crystals had a mesmerising attraction and were undoubtedly capable of storing all sorts of beneficial powers and assisting with freeflow, I was more interested in the guy selling them. I wondered what sort of life he lived, if he was in a relationship, how he felt when he woke up in the morning, what he had for breakfast and what his digestion was like. Our eyes met briefly, I could sense that he was also assessing me. I nodded to him to acknowledge our brief but insightful contact and then cruised along with the crowd.

Rainbow colours attracted my attention again but this time it was brightly coloured images of the Chakras. I had arrived at a stand that focused on creating energy freeflow by balancing the Chakras, or energy centres in the body. Two middle-aged women in blue uniforms were working around massage tables in the centre of the stand. They were in the middle of a therapy session and were holding their hands over the bodies on the tables. The recipients of this treatment seemed very subdued.

One of the workers caught my attention but once again my interest was of a more earthly nature. I found myself wondering what kind of car she drove, what sort of relationship she had with her husband and whether she gave him regular Chakra balances. Her face was serene but I wondered if she ever got angry. I remembered a patient of mine, a nun, who had the same calm expression but swore like a trooper during Bodywork!

Psychics

As I rounded the corner into the next aisle, I found myself staring straight into the penetrating gaze of a psychic. Black gothic lettering over the stall described her as a psychic artist who drew people's spiritual guides and passed on important messages from the invisible worlds. I had been to some great psychics in the past and it too can be an exhilarating freeflow experience. This is because if you are worried about things in your life or are stuck re-living events of the past, it creates negative emotions such as fear which block the flow of Chi in the body. A good psychic can provide instant insight into the issues that have been concerning you and this generates a tremendous sense of relief and stimulates freeflow again. I could feel the woman's psychic power affecting my mind and my energy centres, even from a distance. It was as if she had touched some hidden part of myself, making me feel instantly raw and exposed. Deciding it was better not to imagine any of her personal life, I kept going.

Sugar and caffeine

A sign for organic ice-cream distracted me by engaging me on a purely physical level. Although I liked the idea of having an ice-cream, as a result of my training in health and nutrition I knew that my response to a stimulus of this nature would more likely end in long-term energy loss for short-term satisfaction. The high sugar levels in ice-cream flood the system creating a Chi flow experience which temporarily makes you feel good. However, ice-cream is what I would categorise as an 'anti-food', a product in which the energetic cost to the body of processing it exceeds any nutritional value it might offer.

No, I didn't need ice-cream, I needed a coffee. I tried to order one but the vendor could only offer me coffee-flavoured ice-cream. My interest increased slightly but when he proudly pointed out that it was made from decaffeinated coffee he lost me for good. He must have noticed my disappointment, because he said, 'Mate, this is a health fair, I don't know where you get drugs like caffeine here'. I told him that I had given a talk on much heavier drugs that morning that had attracted a lot of interest. He just laughed and wished me luck.

The ambient noise was overwhelming. Each stand was playing different music and there were performances on stages throughout the hall as well. I passed one of the smaller stages on which a woman in a floating green gown was singing in an angelic voice. Fifty metres further on was a stage with a Kung-fu demonstration and bamboo flute music. Although everything I saw was interesting, all I really wanted now was to sit somewhere in peace for a few minutes. I kept walking in the direction I hoped led towards the coffee shop, passing stands for health foods, jewellery, meditation and yoga, all vying to out-do each other visually to catch the passing trade.

I began to feel a bit overloaded from the sights, sounds and metaphysical concepts that bombarded me from every side. Instinctively, I started planting my feet firmly and consciously on the floor and I made my breathing deep and slow. The feelings of being off-centre faded and I found myself at the entrance to the café. I went straight to the counter and ordered a strong cappuccino. Within minutes, the caffeine entered my system and I felt instantly invigorated. Caffeine, like cocaine, is a stimulant drug and it is the most commonly consumed stimulant drug in the world (Frishman et al. 2003). Caffeine increases the heart rate and makes the Chi flow so, like all other enjoyable things, it too is a freeflow agent but compared to cocaine, a relatively harmless one. With that in mind I decided to have another.

I leaned back in my chair and looked out at the vista of stands all selling techniques or products aimed at generating freeflow. But, like coffee, there is a big difference between 'instant' and the real thing and many on offer were instant. I took another sip of my coffee and decided to forget about philosophising and enjoy my legal freeflow stimulant.

CHAPTER TWO

Marijuana

MY FIRST JOINT

Before I even took drugs, I was convinced that there were
worlds beyond the material one. As a teenager, the walls
of my bedroom were plastered with Roger Dean's fantasy
posters and album covers and I used to spend hours lying
on my bed staring at his magical landscapes of floating
cities, weird plants and fantastical creatures. I would often
walk in the forest by myself imagining its mystical elements. The trees seemed to have personalities, and I could
sense the presence of other beings around me: elves, wizards,
fairies.

33

Whenever I tried to talk about these things to family members though, every conversation ended with them telling me that there were 'no other dimensions, no life after death', and that I should 'stop dreaming and grow up'. I didn't want to, so instead I stopped speaking about it. I couldn't understand why I was so different from the rest of them. A feeling of emptiness grew inside me, as if an important part of myself was missing. The day I smoked my first hash-laced joint with Stefan, that empty feeling completely disappeared and I saw that my dream world could be real.

Stefan was already involved in hippie circles; he had long hair and wore velvet jackets and huge silver rings. He had smoked dope several times and kept telling me how fantastic it was but I hadn't been very interested. I knew nothing about marijuana or other drugs and I was worried about 'losing control' or getting 'addicted'. Stefan convinced me to try it though. He came over one day with a joint and we went to a local park to smoke it. Stefan lit it and then passed it on to me. I liked the taste—it was sweet and herbal—but I wasn't expecting much to happen. Within a few minutes, however, I started to feel the same as I did when I was daydreaming about Roger Dean's images or walking through the forest.

The boring urban park became an inspiring and exciting environment that I wanted to explore. We laughed, swung on the swings, climbed trees and lay on the grass and talked about life. Everything we did had a dreamlike quality to it, but it was also really happening. I felt like a door to a magical and sacred world had opened up in front of me and nothing was going to stop me going through. Chasing that state became my only goal from then on.

MARIJUANA, HASHISH AND FREEFLOW

I set up an offering table in the corner of my room and covered it with statues, incense burners and anything that looked mystical or Eastern. I would smoke hashish in front of it and play Pink Floyd records at full volume. My inner life took on a whole new dimension but this just created more problems with my family. Initially, it wasn't so much the drugs or even the loud music they objected to, but my claim that the drugs made me feel real and that everything else was unreal and that there was a sacred aspect to what I was doing. I had the fervour of a convert which only made matters worse and, as they became increasingly frustrated with me, their words became more scathing and hurtful. This in turn drove me further and further away from them.

After a while I started to think of marijuana as a 'friend' or a medication to alleviate the pain caused by rigid social conditioning. Marijuana made me feel happy and accepted and when I was stoned I could forget the disapproval and criticism of my family. I found myself wanting to feel that way more and more often, so I smoked more frequently. The sense of ceremony, the incense and ritual fell by the wayside, and I ended up getting stoned just about every day.

Naturally, the friction with my family intensified. Now, as well as being 'immature' and a 'dreamer', they also saw me as a 'hopeless drug addict'. I couldn't understand their attitude though. If I had got roaring drunk every night at the pub and brawled or vomited my way home like everyone else did it would have been perfectly acceptable, but if I sat in my room listening to music, smoking a joint and imagining a world founded on peace and love, apparently there was something wrong with me. I knew marijuana was illegal, but I also knew it was nowhere near as dangerous as alcohol. But when I tried to explain this they just wouldn't listen.

CANNABIS

Cannabis in leaf form (marijuana), or resin and oil forms (hash), is currently the most widely produced, trafficked and consumed illicit drug worldwide. Cannabis has a long history of mind-altering as well as practical (e.g. fibre production) and medicinal uses. By the latter half of the 19th century, in Britain and the USA, cannabis-based medications were common and could be purchased freely without prescription. When these products were replaced by the more reliable synthetic drugs (Booth 2003, pp. 94–97), the 'recreational' use of cannabis slowly increased, particularly in the USA, until by 1975 it was the main recreational narcotic used in the West (Booth 2003, p. 240). The 1961 UN Convention on Narcotic Drugs, the first international agreement on the broad classification of drugs into categories, or schedules, classified cannabis, along with heroin, as Schedule IV drugs—those considered to be the most dangerous substances, with high potential for addiction and extremely limited medical value.

The schedules from the 1961 Convention on Narcotic Drugs, and those from the 1971 Convention on Psychotropic Drugs (such as LSD, ecstasy and mescaline) formed the basis for the drafting of consistent legislation in different countries. As an outcome of these and later conferences on illicit traffic in narcotic drugs and psychotropic substances, many countries made cannabis illegal. However, this seems to have had little impact—it is now under cultivation in over 140 countries. In 2002, over 5800 tons of cannabis products were seized globally, including over 4700 tons of marijuana, more than 1000 tons of hashish and over a ton of hash oil (UNODC 2004).

MARIJUANA, ALCOHOL AND THE MYTH OF THE HARMLESS DRUG

Back in the 1970s I really believed that marijuana was harmless compared to alcohol. Even after I had my last joint I continued to believe it, and statistics appeared to support my case. No deaths had ever been recorded from overdosing on marijuana. In fact, one researcher estimated that it would take 800 joints to kill you, but your death would be a result of carbon monoxide rather than cannabinoid poisoning. By comparison, 300 millilitres of vodka could be lethal (Booth 2003, p. 13). It wasn't until I became a practitioner and lecturer in Traditional Chinese Medicine in the 1990s that I revised my opinions on marijuana being harmless, and subsequently on the claim that marijuana was not as bad as alcohol.

An acupuncture seminar presented by Dr Leon Hammer, a renowned practitioner and theoretician, was the turning point for me. During the seminar, while discussing pulse diagnosis— a fundamental diagnostic technique in TCM—Dr Hammer stated that he had observed a connection between a Liver-associated pulse quality and excessive marijuana use. It was the first time I had heard illicit drugs mentioned in the context of Traditional Chinese Medicine and I was immediately interested. Unfortunately he said no more on the topic, but for days afterwards I couldn't stop thinking about it. It stood to reason that if marijuana affected the Liver, which in TCM is connected to the dual functions of 'advance and act' and 'retreat and wait', it might explain things like the lack of motivation that affected many long-term marijuana users.

I wanted to know more but I couldn't find direct references to illicit substance abuse and particular organ conditions or imbalances in standard TCM texts, so I started doing primary source research. The subsequent analysis of my case notes of long-term users revealed symptoms and behavioural patterns linked to imbalances in the Liver. Marijuana was obviously not a harmless drug.

GATEWAY DRUG CYCLE

It turned out that so many of my students had used marijuana that I started including drug references in some of my lectures as a way of explaining the concept of Chi flow or describing certain organ conditions. In one lecture, as I was speaking about the effects marijuana had on the Liver, for some reason I followed it up by explaining how you would need a stimulant drug like speed to override the imbalances caused by the marijuana, and then eventually heroin to override the imbalances caused by the speed. As I talked I scribbled notes on the board and drew diagrams of the affected organs. When I finished I put the pen down and stared at the board. In front of me, written in my own hand, was a logical explanation of the gateway drug cycle.

I was a bit shocked by what I had done. By now I was convinced that long-term marijuana use was certainly not harmless but I still thought the 'gateway drug' theory, in which a soft drug like marijuana could supposedly lead you to hard drug addiction, was propaganda based on ignorance and designed to stop dope-smokers enjoying themselves. The whole gateway concept had always seemed deeply flawed to me. For example, if marijuana really could lead to hard drugs, as the theory proposed, why had millions of marijuana users not all turned into heroin addicts?

Now that Traditional Chinese Medicine had given me a vocabulary to explain the gateway drug cycle and counter all the arguments I had used to discredit the theory, everything changed. It made me think more about drugs from the perspective of their effects on the organs and the Human Energy Field. I combined my empirical knowledge of drugs with the theories of TCM and my research into Energy medicine, and developed a theoretical framework that could make sense of every weird or blissful feeling I had ever had on drugs. I could now explain the attraction of drugs, the mechanisms drugs exploit to make you feel good, and why you would pay for all those good times later on.

TCM also revealed that there were powerful energetic forces behind life and a gateway to 'the invisible world'. This reminded me that my own drug use had also been motivated by my fascination with other dimensions. I had thought that illicit drugs were the only way to access these, but TCM had shown me that not only were there other ways to feel good, but that there were other ways to investigate and interact with the unseen world.

As soon as I had this insight, drugs came back into my life again but in a different way. I found that I was attracting more and more patients and students who either wanted to know about the effects of illicit drugs or had developed conditions related to their drug use. Then I was invited to participate in a government-sponsored program using acupuncture to treat heroin addiction. By the end of that project, my theory that drugs were a way to access a mechanism that was already within all of us had become more resolved.

DRUG RECOVERY PROJECT

My first patient arrived at the treatment centre on a Harley Davidson. He parked on the footpath in front of the clinic and the distinctive throb of the engine reverberated through the building. A hush fell over the reception area as he came through the front door. He was nearly two metres tall and was dressed in black leather pants and a fringed black leather vest with a skull stitched on the back of it. He had a waist-length plait of black hair, a black moustache and goatee, and tattoos covering his arms and chest. Even though his eyes were hidden behind dark lenses, no-one in the waiting room was game to look directly at him. It was like a scene from some old Western movie.

I took him to the treatment room and he told me that he had just kicked a ten-year heroin habit. He had been without a shot for three days and was experiencing the typical signs and symptoms of cold turkey, such as shaky hands and stomach cramps. I could tell that he didn't expect much from me or the program, but he was desperate to stay clean and willing to try anything. I asked him to lie on the table. I used my Chi-training to get myself into the correct state to add extra impact to the acupuncture, and I put the needles into the relevant points.

As I expected, his tremor stopped, his breathing became regular and his stomach cramps eased. He looked at me in total astonishment gasping, 'What the fuck did you put on the needle, eh? Morphine? What's going on man, I'm feeling something like a rush?'

I showed him a sealed packet of acupuncture needles saying, 'The needles I used are completely clean, it's where I put them and what I do with them that is responsible for your rush.'

The guy looked as tough as nails but I could sense that he was really in tune with his inner self and ready to make change. After about twenty minutes I took the needles out and he got up and put his vest back on. He looked at me still amazed. He spoke softly. 'Man, what happened? How can I repeat this? Can you give me some of those needles, I'm going to take them home and bliss out on nothing!'

The one person you can't fool regarding pleasure is a heroin addict. Their world is black and white. There are only two states. They are either on drugs or in extreme discomfort. The biker simply couldn't believe that he could be in a pain-free state without the heroin. I explained to him that what he had been chasing with drugs was not coming from the drugs themselves, but from what they were doing to his Chi flow and his organs. The highs he had experienced before were natural but were artificially triggered. My acupuncture treatment allowed his Chi to flow freely again and correct organ imbalances, a mild version of what the heroin did for him, but he wasn't going to 'come down' afterwards.

He had never heard anything like this before and we ended up discussing different drugs, how they made you feel and the mechanics of freeflow. This same conversation was repeated over and over again with the other participants in the program. Another recurring theme in practically every discussion was the old 'drugs are not as bad as alcohol' claim. The program participants were all ex-heroin addicts, and even though the heroin had proved destructive in terms of their health and happiness, many still believed that heroin was not as bad as alcohol. All believed that marijuana wasn't even a 'real drug' and definitely harmless compared to alcohol.

Over the years I have had this same conversation scores of times, particularly with patients and students who deliberately chose marijuana rather than alcohol in the belief that it was less harmful or that it had no side effects. I have to say that, even as an ex-drug user, I am surprised by just how many people now think like this. In my hippie days, the idea that marijuana was either not harmful or less harmful than alcohol was certainly not mainstream.

A study done in the USA in 1968 estimated that it was less than 0.2 percent of the population who were somehow affiliated with the hippie movement and, by default, the use of marijuana (Booth 2003, p. 214). In Germany at that time it was probably even less. In my school, there were only two kids who had ever tried dope. But in many places marijuana is practically socially acceptable now. In Australia some surveys indicate that at least half the population has experimented with cannabis. Based on my experience I think the actual number could be even higher. This would also account for the widening belief across such a broad spectrum of ages and backgrounds—from successful middle-aged business men to young people—that marijuana is harmless.

MARIJUANA AND ALCOHOL COMPARED

Roger, a young patient of mine, was a good example of someone who truly believed in marijuana's harmless nature. I remember his case clearly because we had some terrific conversations about marijuana and health, but also because he reminded me so strongly of my friend Stefan. Like Stefan, Roger was tall and lithe with long black hair and lively, dark brown eyes. He was also a musician and even dressed in a similar style to the way Stefan had, but with a more contemporary edge. Roger had a large Yin and Yang tattoo on his left arm and a dope leaf on his right: the same symbols that Stefan and I had painted on my Kombi van all those years ago.

Roger was also memorable because, rather than presenting symptoms and seeking diagnosis, he wanted proof that there was nothing wrong with him! He had come to see me because his mother was convinced that he had a problem with marijuana and basically, he wanted to prove her wrong. He had done some subjects at the college where I taught and had heard that I specialised in drugs. He was hoping I could somehow assess his health and give him a report stating that marijuana had not affected him in anyway. He also wanted me to back up his claims that marijuana was harmless and might in fact, in his case, actually be beneficial. He believed that dope helped him to write better songs and play better music. This in turn would improve his career prospects.

Apparently, he had been trying to convince his mother of this but she wouldn't have a bar of it. She would regularly give him newspaper articles which claimed that marijuana was harmful and could lead to psychological breakdown, depression or even to harder drugs. She was convinced that Roger was going to turn into a madman and start rampaging around the house with an axe or something. As far as Roger was concerned though, the articles were simply fear-mongering and the people who had written them had obviously never smoked a joint in their lives or they couldn't have written such crap about it.

Roger thought that the newspapers should have been writing about alcohol, not dope. His father regularly drank to excess, returned home in a violent mood and took out his aggression on Roger's mum. She would then drink to deal with her pain. They were trapped in an alcohol-fuelled cycle of violence and guilt. Roger hated what he saw as his mother's hypocrisy in drinking gin and tonics until she was 'totally rotten' but refusing to listen to his argument that alcohol was a more dangerous drug than marijuana, because alcohol made people violent and abusive but marijuana made people mellow and happy.

Although I would once have wholeheartedly agreed with Roger, a decade of research had made me understand that marijuana and alcohol have such different effects on your Chi and organs that arguing over which was worse was probably not productive. Alcohol is like a food—it has calories and some beverages even have nutritional value. So alcohol can fuel the body and provide energy. If you have a few drinks and then get up on the dance floor you are using the energy the alcohol has provided.

Alcohol can be very destructive, but Western medicine recognises that, unlike the other substances of abuse, there are health benefits associated with moderate alcohol use (Frishman et al. 2003). Illicit drugs, however, have no calories and no nutritional value. If you take ecstasy and dance all night, the energy is drawn from your own inner store and there will be a price to pay later. With drugs it is literally all 'smoke and mirrors'—they force action but do not support it.

Another major difference between marijuana and alcohol that makes them difficult to compare is that alcohol has been an intrinsic part of human culture for thousands of years. Some recent scientific research suggests that an attraction to ethanol may even lie much deeper in our evolutionary past as it may have been a significant part of the pre-human diet. The theory proposes that our fruit-dependant primate ancestors possibly developed an attraction to the ethanol that spikes very ripe fruit, as the smell of ethanol acted as an indictor of where ripe fruit was. In addition, because alcohol stimulates appetite, when they did find the fruit they could then consume more (Kaesuk Yoon 2004).

When I related this idea to Roger he laughed and said that that must have been where the term 'party animal' came from.

Marijuana as a recreational drug is comparatively new to the human species and we have not adapted to it as we have to alcohol. There is, for example, no concept of what a 'safe dose' might be. Potency varies greatly and marijuana can generate what seem to be unpredictable effects. In 1942 in the USA, the OSS, the forerunner of the CIA, investigated the possibility of using marijuana as a truth drug but, when tested, subjects 'broke out in peals of laughter, talked incessantly, became paranoid or clammed up', so the research was abandoned (Booth 2003, p. 160).

From a scientific perspective this unpredictability is thought to stem from the sheer variability of the cannabinoid content in different plants depending on the type of plant, conditions of cultivation and so on (Sarafin et al. 1999), but that does not explain why, when several people share the same joint in which the potency is uniform, it too can deliver a bewildering range of effects. The inability to satisfactorily explain such things was probably one of the reasons why mainstream articles about marijuana being dangerous never rang true for Roger. To explain marijuana's effects fully you would need to look at the physical, emotional and spiritual implications of its use.

MARIJUANA INTERPRETED USING TRADITIONAL CHINESE MEDICINE

TCM employs an entirely different approach to understanding the human body than Western medicine. It makes no distinction between body, mind and spirit so it has a vocabulary capable of being employed to explain the paradoxical aspects of marijuana, its potential as a gateway drug to stimulants and heroin, and how it could have a detrimental effect on 'mental health'. Based on my experience as an ex-drug user and a practitioner of Traditional Chinese Medicine, I would probably have to agree with the claims made in the articles that Roger's mother had given him: that marijuana is definitely not a harmless drug.

I remember Roger being really taken aback by this and immediately asking why, if marijuana was supposed to be so harmful, there were no side effects. He claimed that after a night 'bonging on', he was fine the next day, but after a night drinking he would lose entire days vomiting, hung-over, and unable to function. And his friends were the same! They all smoked marijuana regularly, with no side effects, and they hadn't moved on to harder drugs, so where was the evidence that it was harmful?

Roger had studied enough TCM subjects to be familiar with the basic concepts, so I was able to go into more depth than I would have normally. I explained that even if you perceive yourself as being unaffected, marijuana still disrupts the delicate balance of the Human Energy Field and this is going to have an effect on you one way or another, sooner or later. So, it is not that marijuana has no side effects, but rather that the side effects are complex, subtle and cumulative. They creep up on you over time. Depending on what is termed your 'constitution', this process can be so slow that no cause and effect connection between the symptoms and the drug is ever made. This is one of the reasons so many people believe it is harmless.

I could see that Roger was torn between not really wanting to hear this and wanting to know more. The latter obviously won out because he then said that all his life he had been told that drugs were bad, but when he first tried marijuana he felt unbelievably good. So, if it was supposed to be so bad for him, why did it make him feel so good?

Feeling pleasantly stoned

It was a good question and one that comes up frequently. I too had been told that marijuana was bad, and yet had had the opposite experience when I smoked that first joint. I loved these conversations.

Based on my fusion of TCM, Energy medicine, and Body-Mind therapy, I believe that each drug has a different property and works via particular organs. Marijuana has a magnifying property and it operates primarily via the Liver. The Liver is responsible for a smooth flow of Chi throughout the body (Maciocia 1989, p. 227). So, under the influence of marijuana, you can get a heightened awareness of the Chi flowing. You may experience this as a warm and pleasant sensation which spreads throughout the body and can be particularly strong in the abdominal area where the Liver is located. The feeling can sometimes be so intense in this region that you burst into spontaneous laughter, as you would if someone tickled you in that spot. Because the Chi is flowing smoothly, you feel content, happy and relaxed.

The munchies

As the Chi flows throughout the body, it indirectly amplifies the function of the other organs too. When Stomach and Spleen function is enhanced you can get the munchies, or an insatiable urge to eat, particularly sweet and creamy foods as they resonate with the Spleen. You also have such a heightened sense of taste that a humble toasted sandwich can taste better than a gourmet meal from a five-star restaurant.

As well as enhancing tactile sensations, the freeflowing Chi also amplifies the function of the Kidneys so sexual activities and orgasms can seem much more intense too.

Marijuana and enhanced creativity

The emergence of what you think are brilliant ideas when you are stoned, or feeling more creative, or thinking you are playing better music, all occur because the magnifying property of marijuana has also allowed an increased awareness of 'birth, growth and expansion', which are considered in TCM to be qualities or values associated with the Liver.

Not so pleasantly stoned

Of course not everyone has these pleasant experiences from using marijuana. Some people feel paranoia, paralysing self-consciousness or extreme timidity. This is because they have a different constitution. Traditional Chinese Medicine is based on the concept of duality. The terms Yin and Yang describe this duality and are applied to everything from the macroscopic to microscopic. Marijuana is primarily a Yin drug so if you have a more Yin or passive constitution, it can amplify these qualities and make you feel like you have come to a halt both physically and psychologically. In this state, even the smallest, simplest task seems impossibly huge and you are unable to do anything but sit and stare blankly into space.

This zombie-like condition can be described as Liver Yin excess. It can be a suffocating experience because in that state, due to Yin dominance, you are unable to access the Liver Yang necessary for physical or even psychological movement. This makes you feel helpless. Liver Yin excess is like the feeling you get in those dreams where something nasty or scary is chasing you but when you try to run, you can't move because you are stuck in quicksand or cement. If marijuana has this effect on you but you keep using it, it can create the environment in which marijuana leads to harder drugs.

☯ CASE STUDY: MARIJUANA AND LIVER YIN EXCESS

I had another patient, Scotty, who would end up in this Liver Yin excess state when he smoked dope and this eventually led him to heroin addiction. In the early days, when he and his friends first discovered marijuana, everything was great. Marijuana made life exciting, so they used it every day. After about a year of this, Scotty found himself unable to interact with his friends when he was stoned. He would sit around staring blankly at nothing in particular while everything went on around him.

Even though he kept getting trapped in this state he didn't want to stop smoking dope because if he wasn't stoned he wouldn't be part of the group dynamic. He hoped that the problem would pass but it became worse each time, eventually making him feel isolated and different. He became paranoid that if his friends knew how he was feeling they would think that there was something wrong with him, so he kept a smile fixed on his face as if he was having a good time.

But in a Liver Yin excess state, you are not having a good time. The feeling is extremely unpleasant, as it not only makes you incapable of normal social interaction, but it also generates this constant nagging feeling that something is 'missing'. This is because in a Liver Yin excess state you are governed by the Yin quality of 'retreat and wait', which is the Liver's mechanism for introspection. So what you are missing is Liver Yang, which generates 'advance and act', the Liver's mechanism by which you move forward in life and engage with your environment.

Combining alcohol and marijuana

In Scotty's case, he just wanted the weird feelings to go away and he searched for a substance that would make this happen. He discovered that drinking alcohol when he was stoned could liven things up for him. Alcohol forces a rise of Liver Yang which boosts the 'advance and act' function of the Liver. Accordingly, it made being stoned more active and thus more enjoyable for Scotty. His drink of choice was rum and coke, which added a massive sugar hit to the mix and really got the Yang up and stimulated the 'advance and act' mechanism.

It is this same property of alcohol that can make overtly Yang constitutional types with suppressed anger suddenly become violent when they drink. When the surge of Yang from the alcohol hits the Liver it can drive them to 'advance and act'. It is an almost involuntary, primal response. Marijuana, however, has the opposite effect. Under its influence even an aggressive or Yang person is eventually affected primarily by the Liver's function of 'retreat and wait', so they become more passive than active. This is another reason why so many people think that marijuana is less dangerous than alcohol. When I was involved in counselling work, even the police would say that they would rather deal with a mob of stoned people than a single violent drunk.

In one of my discussions with Roger he had told me bitterly that he wished his dad would smoke dope rather than drink so he could 'mellow out' instead of being so aggressive. But as I explained to Roger, marijuana cannot be used to counter anger or stress because it increases rather than corrects the underlying imbalances in the Human Energy Field that have caused the anger or stress in the first place. If, for example, his dad smoked marijuana it could temporarily enhance Liver Yin qualities. This would allow him to look at life without needing to participate in it, so nothing would trigger his anger. But, if he had an imbalance of Liver Yang from, say, years of suppressed anger, when the effects of the marijuana wore off he would be even more aware of how annoying everything was, so dope would just make him more irritable and angry in the long run.

For Scotty though, alcohol allowed him to interact with his friends again while he was stoned. Unfortunately, because his Yin constitution couldn't handle such a potent mix, he was only able to maintain his active state for about an hour before passing out on the nearest couch, chair or floor.

Then he tried speed and thought he had solved the problem.

On speed everything felt exciting and entertaining again, like it had in the old days. It could instantly transform him from a zombie into a social, active and communicative person. He thought that speed allowed him to become the person he had always wanted to be and he didn't ever want to go back to how he felt before. He wanted to take speed for the rest of his life. But feeling good on speed has a limited life. It is just a matter of time until it peaks in terms of pleasure and the side effects become very bad. From there, the only drug left that can create the impression of organ balance again is heroin and Scotty finally became a heroin addict. For him, marijuana really did lead to heroin.

MARIJUANA: THE YIN DRUG

Marijuana has less immediate impact on people such as Roger, who have a primarily Yang constitution. These people are quick to interact and engage with others and often initiate contact and conversation. From the moment Roger walked into my clinic he was engaging and extroverted, a classic indicator of 'advance and act', whereas Scotty, who had a primarily Yin constitution, did not initiate conversation and responded only to direct questions.

Either way though, because marijuana is primarily a Yin drug, 'advance and act' will eventually be replaced by 'retreat and wait' in both a short- and long-term context. In the short term, as the marijuana begins to take effect, it can make the user feel temporarily motivated and vigorous but after a period of time, even people like Roger end up sitting around doing nothing. They are not in a Liver Yin excess state, as they are not experiencing emotional torment, but it is no longer an exciting or active state either. It is somewhere in between. It is waiting, but waiting without anticipation.

In the long term, this lethargy and passivity previews the kind of state that marijuana use can create on a more permanent basis. This is why many regular dope-smokers find they need alcohol to liven things up. In a 1998 study of 200 long-term marijuana users in Australia, it was found that more than half were also consuming alcohol at hazardous or harmful levels (Swift et al. 1998). As marijuana primarily impacts upon the Liver, the more frequently it is used, the more quickly the person progresses towards either passivity or frustration and cynicism, both symptoms of imbalances in the Liver.

Most people are familiar with the stereotypical image of the ageing hippie or heavy dope smoker who can't ever get their act together and do anything. This is not a personality type as many people think, it is often a behaviour arising from imbalances caused by excessive marijuana use. In Traditional Chinese Medicine this condition can be described as Liver Yang deficiency. Unfortunately, the majority of long-term marijuana users will eventually fall into this category. It is such a slow and insidious process though, that they won't see it happening. They will just change slowly over time until they eventually forget how active, engaging and energetic they once were.

The speed at which this change occurs is dictated by drug intake but also by levels of Jing, the essence which in TCM is thought to determine basic constitutional strength and vitality. People with a predominantly Yang constitution, strong Jing and a disciplined and focused lifestyle—which assists in the cultivation of Liver Yang—can regularly use marijuana and remain active and creative for years, maybe even decades. However, even for them, marijuana will slowly deplete Liver Yang and subsequently affect their ability to act upon their ideas.

It is this effect of the drug that can make people become 'talkers' rather than 'doers'. Once this happens, the magnifying nature of the drug, rather than increasing awareness of growth or expansion, increases awareness of being stagnant physically and emotionally. In this state, evidence of 'advance and act' in other people can make the drug-user acutely aware of their own deficiencies and they can become emotionally reactive.

Marijuana, emotional reactivity and talking not doing

Reactive behaviour could be described as making involuntary and inappropriate emotional responses to certain stimuli. During our discussions on reactivity and marijuana, Roger told me about someone he knew, Rachel, who was 'stoned all the time'. He said she was always talking about things she was going to do, like writing a script or starting a production company, but she never did anything. No one paid much attention to her when she talked about her ideas because they all knew that it was just talk. Rachel would get really upset about that though, and she constantly attacked other people's successes. For example, when Roger's girlfriend got offered a great job modelling swimwear on a yacht, Rachel immediately made some catty remark about not needing brains to do a job like that. This sounded very much as though evidence of 'advance and act' in someone else was triggering emotional pain in Rachel, probably due to Liver Yang deficiency, which she dealt with by immediately lashing out at the trigger.

Anger ensures that Chi keeps moving; if you get angry about something you are stimulated to do something about it, to make something change. This is how great human rights movements begin. However, it is too easy to use anger to lash out at others, which temporarily alleviates feelings of stagnation, pain or frustration. The challenge is to transform anger and thus, use it as an opportunity for personal growth instead.

Roger also told me about a time when his band had played as the support act for a well known group. Roger had given Rachel a back-stage pass and after the show she immediately approached the lead singer of the main act, telling him that she wanted to make a documentary about his band. The guy was interested and thought she was serious, so he took her phone number. Roger was furious when he found out, because he knew Rachel would not follow up on it and in the end it would make him look bad because he was the one who gave her the backstage pass.

I could understand Roger's annoyance but, as I explained to him, we all need to experience movement and growth to be happy so it is natural to want to do things with our skills or ideas. However, if you are a creative or talented person who has become Liver Yang deficient, as Rachel may have done, you still have your creativity but you have lost your ability to act.

Everyone has a mental picture of who they are, of who they want to be and what they want to do in life. In TCM this is directly connected with the Liver. If you repeatedly take a substance that has a direct impact on the functioning of the Liver, as marijuana does, it can create an imbalance between your visions or ideas, and the impetus to act upon them. The idea becomes bigger and the action becomes smaller so you become more occupied with thinking and talking than doing. You become a 'talker' not a 'doer'. It is as if you become stuck on a loop and keep repeating the first part of the process over and over again.

You would still speak enthusiastically about each new idea, as if you were really going to do it, because that creates a temporary sense of progress or action. But for this talk to be a satisfying experience, you need feedback from the other party. Without this the Chi won't flow and the Liver manifests frustration. This was why Rachel would get upset when Roger and his friends ignored her ideas, but also why she would enthusiastically pitch projects to strangers. They believed she would follow through on the talk so they would engage with her ideas. Of course it is not just heavy marijuana use that can create these behaviours. I have had plenty of patients who behaved in a similar manner for all sorts of reasons, from constitutional conditions to organ dysfunction.

Roger said that he thought that was all very well in theory, but personally he felt like telling Rachel to 'piss off' every time he saw her. He only put up with her because she was going out with a mate of his. But, as I pointed out to him, he didn't tell her to 'piss off'. This is because he had a choice, and each time he saw her he chose not to. His organs were probably functioning better than Rachel's, and he was experiencing growth and development in his own life. However, once imbalances in the organs and Energy Field reach a certain stage, you no longer have that kind of emotional choice.

TCM is a preventative medicine, which means it can predict the outcome of certain actions. If Roger kept smoking marijuana at the rate he currently did, it would only be a matter of time before he too was like Rachel. As horrified as he would be at the thought, he was heading down the same path and would never see it happening.

☯ CASE STUDY: MARIJUANA, CYNICISM AND FRUSTRATION

I have had many patients whose behaviour was, unbeknownst to them, gradually being altered by the imbalances that heavy marijuana use created in the Liver. One of these, Steve, was a mechanic who had smoked dope daily for years because he was bored with the mindless and repetitive nature of his job.

Woodworking was his true passion and he spent all his free time in his workshop at home designing and building pieces of furniture.

At the age of forty, he decided to change his life and make furniture production his new profession. Now that it was no longer a hobby though, he felt under pressure to succeed so he smoked even more marijuana than usual to stimulate creativity and manage stress. Eventually, lacking Liver Yang for 'advance and act', he found it increasingly difficult to get projects either underway or completed. As the months passed he fell behind schedule and started working later and later into the night. Each morning he felt sluggish and uninspired and would usually spend a few hours sharpening his tools or rearranging things in his workshop before smoking a joint and going back to the drawing board. Then he would lose himself in the mental process of designing again.

On the occasions when he did get his designs off the drawing board, he would become obsessed by the idea of perfection and would try to make one component of the piece as perfect as possible. This was the result of the 'magnifying property' of the drug, which, combined with the unavailability of Yang for 'advance and act', virtually froze him to one place. What should have been six-week commissions dragged on for months. Then, when he finally did deliver the pieces, the clients were usually so annoyed by all the delays that there was no positive feedback.

However, because the marijuana had altered his sense of time, Steve couldn't understand why they were upset and after a few repeats of this scenario he started thinking that no one appreciated him. He became cynical and bitter. His frustration needed an outlet so he began looking for faults in everything and everyone from politicians to parking inspectors. He constantly criticised everything, including his wife, in an attempt to make her fit into his negative and stagnant view of the world. It wasn't long before their relationship began to suffer.

Trapped in reactive emotionality, he became more and more frustrated and withdrew into himself. Now the magnifying nature of the drug increased his awareness of being stagnant. He decided that he 'deserved' marijuana because the whole world was 'screwed-up' anyway. As far as he was concerned, everything was someone else's fault. Inevitably, he fell into the textbook Liver Yang deficiency depression type which is characterised by 'low-grade irritability, angry withdrawal and muffled agitations, which may be expressed by excessive smoking or overeating' (Hammer 1990, p. 165).

Eventually, he got to the point where he couldn't bear it anymore: his relationship was suffering, his business was in trouble and he felt bad all the time. His wife made an appointment for him to see me. In our first meeting when I asked about his symptoms, he described himself as feeling depressed, stuck in a rut, aimless and frustrated. When we talked about his regular use of marijuana, he said that he knew he smoked a lot of pot but that he didn't think it was a problem. He said that he didn't need it and could stop any time he wanted to.

Many people who are Liver Yang deficient from marijuana use make statements such as this, but in fact it takes a long time for all effects of the drug to leave the Human Energy Field. It is only after two or three years without it that a long-term user can confidently say 'I don't need it'.

Steve was following his dreams by working for himself making furniture, so he felt he should have been happy about his life, but to me, the dope was undermining his happiness.

He had become caught in a cycle where he used marijuana to regulate the flow of Liver Chi, but this simultaneously reduced his ability to implement his ideas, so he would feel the need to smoke more dope. When I asked Steve why he used marijuana he said that in the old days he used to smoke with his mates to have a laugh, but then he kept smoking because he liked the way it made him feel. With a joint he could chill-out, feel mellow and also really get into his design work.

I pointed out that what he had really been doing with the marijuana was implementing change. He was making himself relaxed instead of stressed. He was making himself happy instead of frustrated. It could be said that his intent was to change his state for the better. I believe that anyone who takes drugs of any sort, from aspirin to heroin, does so for this very reason.

Even if you smoke a joint to go and have fun with your friends, it means that you are not perfectly happy with the way you are, otherwise you would not have taken that drug. Wanting to improve or enhance your mood, become more sociable or feel more at ease with others, is still wanting to change your state of being. I always tell dope-smokers who want to quit that taking up marijuana was actually their first step on the path to change. Steve had kept smoking dope because fundamentally, he didn't like the way he felt about himself. He wanted change and dope had become the only method he had to make things feel as if they were different.

After a few appointments with me Steve decided that marijuana was connected to his unhappiness and it was time to give up. It turned out that he had tried to do this before but had found it impossible. He would end up unable to sleep and stressed-out. I explained that simply giving up marijuana would not create the changes he was after. It would in fact remove his only current technique for implementing change and leave him with a big gap in his life as well as the side effects. I suggested that he focus on 'adding' things to improve his health and happiness and thus implement change on a deep level, while gradually reducing his intake of marijuana.

He was comfortable with this approach and I designed a holistic recovery program for him that would create a sense of wellbeing and change through therapy, exercise, meditation and supplements. Because he was Liver Yang deficient, I included a daily session on a treadmill to progressively develop Liver Yang. This is important for recovering marijuana users because each time you undertake endurance exercise you will always hit the point where you don't want to do it. But if you over-ride that and keep going, it requires the Liver function of 'advance and act'. Repeating this develops 'advance and act' until it becomes an ingrained character trait. It becomes part of you.

I also suggested that Steve take up a meditative practice to help him gain references to the freeflow state without the use of drugs. One of the reasons smoking dope is so much fun is the joy, excitement and laughter that it can generate. Constant use of marijuana though, will inevitably stress this function. So a crucial thing to do when you stop using the drug is to repair the mechanism that provides a natural experience of joy and most meditative techniques can do this.

If you don't find a way to get some joy and excitement in your life it is easy to feel not as engaged with life as other people, to feel 'not right' in yourself, or to have the nagging sense of 'missing something'. These feelings are the result of all the imbalances that the marijuana has created in your organs and Energy Field, but if you are not aware of this you will instinctively seek to correct the situation through substances. We all manage ourselves in this way: if we need perking up we might have a coffee, to reduce stress we might have a few drinks, to comfort ourselves we might eat something sweet. In the drug world though, such solutions are often sought via other, more powerful drugs.

CHAPTER THREE

The psychedelic drugs

MOVING UP THE DRUG LADDER

Towards the end of the 1970s, even though the punk, cocaine and speed era had begun, my friends and I were still drawn to the hippie movement and marijuana and hash, the hippie drugs. However, after years of consistent daily use, these drugs were losing their power to make everything seem exciting. We had reached the point where we were stoned every day and hanging around with other long-term dope smokers. We no longer had deep conversations about how we were going to change the world and were more likely to just sit around silently passing bongs or joints—we weren't high anymore; we were just stoned.

On one occasion, a novice joined our group and after just a few puffs on a joint he got really high. He was laughing and excited and wanted to engage with us on that same level but marijuana wasn't having that effect on us anymore and we just found his reaction annoying. We had reached the stage where we had to keep smoking dope because without it we were moody, argumentative and annoyed with each other. For us dope had become a necessity and his innocent enjoyment of it just highlighted how dependant we had become.

I still remember the night this really hit home for me. We had been unable to score but Stefan had a small amount of hash, enough for two of us, so he and I went to his place to smoke it. But then Karl and Dietrich turned up, without any drugs, and Stefan and I were actually really pissed-off with them because it meant we had to share what we had. It was not enough for the four of us to get high so we would all be trapped in our negative emotional states for the whole night.

Of course, Stefan and I would have done the same. We were all in the same boat. If we couldn't score we would go and 'visit' someone who we knew had drugs. We would pretend it was purely social and I would even do things like bring something with me to make it look as if we had a reason to visit, but we all knew differently. At this stage it was no longer recreational because our lives were governed by the action of drugs. The marijuana had depleted our Yang to the point where we couldn't break out of the pattern even if we wanted to. We were trapped.

LSD

To escape we began taking LSD more frequently. LSD is the most powerful of the hallucinogenic or psychedelic drugs. It is at the other end of the spectrum from dope, which pharmacologically is considered as a mild hallucinogen. LSD could take you to other dimensions, open up your soul, allow you to see what the universe was made of. LSD really made you feel as if you were living the dream.

Taking an acid trip was as exciting for us as heading off on an exotic holiday would have been for a non-drug user. LSD could take you way beyond the boundaries of the known world to magical, colourful realms inhabited by fantastical beings. LSD was thrilling, dangerous and mind-blowing all at once. It allowed us to interact again, to move, to express, to share, it made life active again. We needed it, it gave us something to look forward to. A Saturday without acid was like a grey, boring Monday.

LSD

LSD, lysergic acid diethylamide, or 'acid', was first synthesised in 1938 by Swiss chemists seeking a circulatory and respiratory stimulant. In the early 1940s, after the discovery that it was also a potent psychedelic and hallucinogen, medical interest in the drug increased. LSD was seen as a powerful tool for learning about brain–mind relationships, and by the late 1940s it was being prescribed for conditions including heroin dependence, depression and alcoholism (Strassman 2001, pp. 23–27). Its highly publicised use in the hippie movement in the 1960s led to LSD and other similar materials being listed as controlled substances

---

in the 1971 UN Convention on Psychotropic Substances. In terms of ongoing 'recreational' use, LSD and other hallucinogens are much less popular than the stimulant drugs. An Australian survey revealed that in 2002, 1.1 percent of the population (14 years and over) had used hallucinogens. By comparison, 35 percent of 20–29-year-olds had used cannabis (AIHW 2002).

LSD connected us back to our original motivation for taking drugs—our desire for the bliss and exhilaration of altered states. Better still, it belonged to us, to our generation. There was a lot of misinformation being circulated about LSD at the time, from official sources, but we knew more than them. We understood LSD. It was not addictive and it was not something you could die from overdosing on, like you could on heroin. You did not suffer withdrawal symptoms from LSD. Nor did you think you could fly and jump off tall buildings, as reports in the paper suggested. The danger with LSD lay in using too much or stuff that was too strong.

One guy we knew did this. Some people said he took five trips at once, others claimed it was ten. Either way he didn't come back, he got trapped in the hallucinogenic state. He would walk in circles around trees, talk to himself and fall into fits of giggles for no apparent reason. It was impossible to communicate with him because you couldn't hold his attention. He was no longer able to function on planet earth and he had to live with his mother.

We didn't think this would ever happen to us though. We always used reliable sources and we were careful about how much we took. In addition, because a trip could last up to twelve hours and once it started it was nearly impossible to communicate with anyone who was not in the same state, we always had a guide, a non-LSD user who acted as a mediator between the LSD world and the real world. The fact was that LSD could generate such incredible experiences that nothing; not the bad press, nor the pressure from our families, or the stories about what it could do to your brain, made the slightest bit of difference to us.

We were young, we wanted excitement, freedom, joy and spontaneity, not the seriousness and conformity that German society demanded of us. LSD showed us that the obsession with responsibility, money and time was meaningless. On LSD all the rules could be broken. It set our minds and spirits free. On LSD we were no longer even bound by three-dimensional reality as, on occasion, it allowed us to defy the physical laws of the universe.

One of our more memorable experiences of this occurred on an early acid trip. We had dropped the acid in Karl's apartment and, at one point, we all stood together at the window watching people on the street below doing their shopping, walking their dogs or driving their cars. We discussed what we were seeing amongst ourselves. Rudi, our guide, assumed we were hallucinating as we were in reality all standing in front of a blank wall that had no windows. Out of curiosity though, he went outside to look around and discovered that everything we had been seeing and talking about was really there. The people, their pets, their cars; everything. What we saw through our imaginary window was exactly what we would have seen had a window really been there. On that trip, for some reason, LSD allowed us to see right through the wall.

One of the inexplicable things about our LSD use was that every time Dietrich, Karl, Stefan and I took acid together, we all ended up on the same trip. We shared the same visions and experiences and we could also see each other and inter-act in these other worlds. We might not look the same, we might have wildly distorted features or be the wrong colour, but this would all seem perfectly normal at the time. The communal nature of the trip made it a bonding experience for us but it could have a downside as well. With LSD, you had to take it 'at the right time, in the right place, with the right people'. Even then though, the hallucinogenic state could easily switch from good to bad and if one person lost it, everyone else was in danger of going down with them.

Good trips and bad trips

In 1979 when the movie *Alien* came out we had all eagerly gone to see it but the next time we took LSD, during cross-over or onset of the trip, for some reason Dietrich mentioned the scene in which the alien had exploded out of the egg and latched onto the face of the astronaut. As soon as he said the words we all immediately saw that image and for a few incredibly intense minutes, we had to concentrate very hard on not getting trapped in it. It could have easily become reality, a living nightmare in which that alien was attached to our own faces, suffocating us, and twelve hours with the aliens is a long time.

In the early days though, just about every trip was good. We used LSD in a ceremonial and sacred way, as we had once used hashish and marijuana. LSD supported our dreams of being spiritual rather than material beings. But this faded over time, along with the hippie movement and, as the end of the decade approached, we all became more cynical about the hippie dream. It no longer inspired us like it once had but because it was how we had defined ourselves, we took even more LSD to try to recapture a feeling of excitement. But the bad trips began increasing; acid bares your psyche and it can expose every psychological or emotional weakness.

BAD ACID TRIP

It was freezing cold and we huddled together in the damp, dark room. Karl gave me a Red Star and I put it in my mouth. Somewhere in the back of my mind I had some doubt about it. It wasn't the right time or the right place and we didn't have a guide. The moment it touched my tongue I knew it was a mistake, but now there was no going back. I was staring at a flower in a vase on the table which had started to dance, but instead of being excited by the hallucination I felt disillusioned and depressed by it. Some part of me cynically said, 'So what?' Instantly, the walls and ceiling began to close in on me. I panicked. I was trying to breathe but I couldn't feel any oxygen reaching my lungs. Terrified, I ran for the door. My only thought was to get out and get some space.

Karl and Dietrich followed me onto the street where crowds of hideously distorted people with huge elongated noses and receding foreheads leered at us from every side. The houses lining the street turned into luridly coloured castles, brimming with a dark menace. Then the sky and the houses started closing in on us too. Desperately we all ran to my Kombi and I drove frantically out of town. The road swerved and twisted in front of me and I didn't know which side to drive on. The trees whipped past at an alarming speed and the corners came up so fast I was terrified I would miss them. I checked the speedometer but when I saw that I was only doing 20 km/h, I realised that I was tripping out of control.

Shock jolted through me and the steering wheel turned into soft rubber and swung around wildly. I couldn't control the car and it lurched off the road. We abandoned it where it was and walked until we were numb. When we finally got back to the squat, Karl took some Valium and asked me if I wanted any. I desperately wanted that pill but taking it would be like admitting that something wasn't right anymore. So I said no, pretending that the trip was okay, but on the inside, I felt as if the part of me that could make me feel good had been removed.

MESCALINE

Even though the bad trips became more frequent, we didn't consider giving up our search for bliss, we just looked for another drug to generate that state. There were other long-lasting psychedelics around such as 'Serenity, Tranquillity and Peace' or STP, but it had a reputation as a serious, mind-warping, chemical concoction and it was only used by hard-core drug takers. We wanted something that generated warm and spiritual experiences. A friend of Stefan's had taken mescaline a few times and raved about its magical qualities. It was supposed to be far less potent than LSD but we decided to try it anyway.

MESCALINE

Mescaline is a psychedelic substance derived from the Peyote Cactus. Peyote has had a long history of use in South American and Mexican cultures but was little known in the 'recreational drug' context of the West until the 19th century. In the 1890s, German chemists isolated mescaline from peyote but medical interest was limited, possibly because of the nausea and vomiting associated with its use (Strassman 2001, pp. 23–27). As the first psychedelic compound known by Western chemists (Pinchbeck 2003, p. 121), mescaline became a 'benchmark' against which the strength of other psychotropic substances could be measured. For example, LSD is described as being one thousand times the strength of mescaline (Strassman 2001 p. 23). Mescaline was listed as a controlled substance in the 1971 UN Convention on Psychotropic Substances.

MESCALINE TRIP

Stefan gave Rudi, our usual guide, his 'payment' of five amphetamine pills and a block of hash, and then we took the mescaline. There was a sense of anticipation in the air. We had bought the mescaline a couple of days beforehand in Amsterdam, from a reliable source, so we knew it would be good and we had been eagerly looking forward to trying it. The effects started to hit about half an hour later. It had none of the chemical feel or metallic harshness of LSD, it was softer, more natural. It was more a body trip than a head trip.

We decided to go out and Rudi drove us to the forest in my Kombi. We got out of the car and walked until we found a clearing in the trees that was strewn with large boulders. In our collective drug-induced vision it became a magical place. Everything was washed in a hazy grey-blue colour and a heavy, sentient fog drifted in and out of the trees. We could hear an other-worldly shrilling sound around and within us and then a powerful presence made contact and welcomed us to that place.

It was mind-blowingly sacred and we felt inspired to use the rocks to build a huge statue in homage to this presence.

However, when we started to move some of the rocks to form the base, we discovered that our bodies were sheathed by a kind of protective bubble and we were able to lift really big, heavy boulders without effort. They were like cardboard props from a movie set. So instead of building a statue, lifting the rocks became our prime focus and the whole trip then revolved around exploring this amazing phenomenon of zero gravity and zero resistance.

The following morning reality hit. I was so sore I could barely move and I was engulfed by such a heavy sadness that I couldn't stop weeping. A week later when I felt more normal, I went back to the place in the forest only to realise that even with all my strength, I could barely move any of the rocks, let alone lift them.

Mescaline felt much less toxic than LSD, which felt clinical, at times even brutal. During the onset of an LSD trip I often felt as if my brain was being squeezed and distorted in a vice and then forcibly jerked into a new position. It was as if LSD had one role and that was to initiate the trip. Mescaline was a warm and nurturing drug that had a real spiritual depth to it. We were all captivated and wanted more sacred drug experiences. We thought that we had found our replacement for LSD. Unfortunately though, good quality mescaline was extremely hard to get. So we ended up experimenting with various other psychedelic substances and mixtures in our quest to get higher and higher, such as hash cookies laced with magic mushrooms, but nothing could ever recapture the feel of that mescaline trip.

PSYCHEDELICS INTERPRETED USING TRADITIONAL CHINESE MEDICINE

All drugs use the organs as a platform to work from. My research indicates that marijuana primarily affects the Liver and magnifies the actions and conditions of the Liver and its associated opposing emotions of frustration or happiness. Psychedelic drugs such as LSD operate via the Heart which is associated with either joy and bliss or shock and panic. However, in Traditional Chinese Medicine, the Heart has another role; it houses the mental energies and controls all higher mental functions. It is said that the Heart 'stores the mind' (Hammer 1990, p. 175). If you interpret the actions of a psychedelic drug from this perspective, it could be said that it derives its effects from your mind; from how you interpret and react to the hallucinations.

TCM considers hallucinations an extreme of a normal function, a particular form of Yin and Yang disharmony in which the Yang is not confined by the Yin and thoughts run out of control. Long-term hallucinogenic drug use increases the imbalance between Yin and Yang; it separates body and mind. Mind is Yang; it is active, ungraspable, ethereal, invisible and non-substantial. It is fundamentally rootless and is constantly moving and expanding. Yin is substance and the mind is dependant on Yin to provide control, structure and boundaries for it. Yin allows linear, logical and constructive thought. Without Yin the activities of the mind cannot be used productively.

In TCM physical reality is characterised by the union of body, mind and spirit. LSD disturbs that equilibrium and releases the mind from the control of the body. This is why when you take an acid trip, it feels like your mind is explosively set free after years of captivity. You become pure mind, pure thought—nothing can stop you, hold you back or limit you in any way. On LSD you are formed entirely by your perceptions, feelings and beliefs. What you think is what you are, what you feel is who you are.

It is an intoxicating feeling, but the speed at which a good trip can turn bad also makes you realise how fragile the mind is without the control mechanism of the body. The body is like a safety net. It can store emotions and pain and keep them inaccessible from the conscious mind. Hallucinogenic drugs break the bonds that keep your mind in this safe space and suppressed emotions and feelings can be set free instantly.

The five elements

A basic tenet of Traditional Chinese Medicine is that the entire natural world, from the macroscopic to the microscopic, including humankind, consists of five elements: Fire, Earth, Metal, Water and Wood. Every part of the body and every emotion or organ is associated with a specific element. These elements control and nurture each other and you need to keep them in balance for good health. Any drug you take, legal or illegal, will affect this balance.

Because hallucinogens primarily target the Heart they also have an impact on the associated Fire element, which in turn is associated with insight and expression. So if you 'accept' the trip, Chi flows smoothly, the Fire element generates insight and expression, the Heart manifests joy and excitement and you have a blissful experience. Charismatic religious practices, deep meditation, passionate loving sex and intense creativity can also operate in this way.

During the mescaline trip in the forest, even though it was totally outlandish, I felt as if everything was perfectly normal. I felt nurtured by the presence that welcomed me. I believed that I belonged there in that world, it was as familiar to me as home. More importantly though, being in that place and being able to lift those huge rocks as if they were weightless was wildly exciting. I felt no anxiety or mental confusion at onset or at any point during the trip. It never occurred to me that what I was doing and seeing was impossible, so Chi was able to keep flowing, the Fire element and Heart responded accordingly, and the trip remained blissful.

However, all it takes is a hint of mental confusion, resistance or fright to distort or block the flow of Chi and it can instantly set off a bad trip. In my last bad acid trip, I saw that flower dancing on the table but rather than responding with excitement, I resisted. Because I resisted, the flow of Chi was blocked, the Fire element didn't provide insight and expression and nothing made sense to me. Consequently the Heart generated shock, I started freaking out and then the walls closed in on me.

THE BODY–MIND CONNECTION

Acid illustrates the direct connection between the body and mind. You do create your own reality. This is equally applicable in a non-drug context, but in a less obvious manner. If you resist an event in your life the Chi flow is prone to distortion, creating the potential for blockages to form. The more blockages you have the more reactive you become, and negative behaviour patterns will develop. Your life can then go on a downward spiral characterised by an ever-increasing chain of negative occurrences. However, if you meet an event with acceptance, the Chi flows smoothly, no distortions occur, no blockages form and your life will progress on an upward spiral of positivity, excitement and bliss. This is the essence of Body–Mind therapies.

This is just theory though; in reality you can't just decide intellectually to 'accept' stimuli that are perceived as negative. You can't just 'be happy'. You need to train in a technique that allows you to instantaneously transcend the desire to resist. This requires the union of body, mind and spirit, which is where disciplines such as yoga and Tai-chi come into the picture. On acid, you can just decide to 'accept' because the drug has temporarily created a freeflow state.

PSYCHEDELIC DRUGS AND SPIRITUALITY

We were reluctant to give up hallucinogens because a good trip could make us feel like we were an integral part of something much bigger and more meaningful than the boring and restrictive society we were born into. Hallucinogens made us feel that we had a cosmic significance. They allowed some mysticism and magic to enter our grey and rigid world. Life in urban Germany was pretty brutal. I never saw a week without a fight somewhere. Big, burly men would punch the lights out of young teenage boys with no concept of fair play, provocation or 'picking on someone their own size'.

The fear of violence was always present. You could get beaten up by total strangers while waiting at the bus stop, in a pub, a shop or anywhere. I had to go through a park on the way to school and I never knew whether I'd make it without getting attacked. I often arrived at school with black and swollen eyes or split lips. It was a culture in which anger, resentment and aggression were the grounds for interaction. Boys were supposed to be tough so there was no point crying about it. It was a soulless world. We longed for something to feed our spirits and we thought that that was what the psychedelic drugs were doing.

I think that some hallucinogenic trips can give glimpses of our spiritual destiny. Many years after I had taken my last trip I read an article which claimed that although there was a remarkable similarity between the drugs that humans like to abuse and those that laboratory monkeys will self-administer (cocaine, amphetamines, heroin, alcohol, nicotine and opiates), hallucinogens were the only class of drugs preferred only by humans (Friedman 1993). I believe that this is because the glimpse of spiritual or enlightened states that they can evoke is our human destiny and birthright. We recognise this on some level. We long for it.

LSD and therapy

Even in parts of the scientific world, the spiritual aspect of LSD was noted. Initially, when its powerful psychedelic properties were first discovered, it seemed that science had found the tool for understanding the relationship between the human mind and its brain chemistry. After WWII, many research projects were underway in which volunteers, psychiatric patients and people suffering terminal illnesses were administered psychedelic drugs. Remarkable successes were recorded for many conditions, and in the terminally ill drugs such as LSD seemed able to generate major psychological breakthroughs in terms of the subject's ability to accept their condition or address deep-seated, emotionally charged issues with their families (Strassman 2001, pp. 23–29).

As a therapist, regardless of what field you work in, the goal is to try to identify the true emotional state of the patient. In my work, I focus on de-obstructing the blockages in the Human Energy Field where suppressed emotions are stored, thus releasing or revealing the underlying cause of the patient's condition. This can be a lengthy process. LSD, however, can instantly expose every emotion and every thought so it is not surprising that it was thought to have huge therapeutic potential. The context in which it would have been administered would be very different to that of current illicit use though. Firstly, the subject would be under the guidance of a health care professional who would monitor and direct their experience, and secondly, they would probably be administered a much lower dose than that of the illicit drug user.

Finding God

This therapeutic potential of LSD was never fully investigated because the hippie abuse of psychedelic drugs created such a scandal that funding was withdrawn from all psychedelic research. The connection between spirituality and psychedelic drugs remained though. Dr Rick Strassman, who initiated the renewal of human psychedelic research in 1990 using DMT, a powerful psychedelic which is actually produced in the body, believed that the drug could be taken in a religious context to experience a deeper relationship with the divine.

Once I would have agreed. There were times when I reached such heights on acid that I felt I was in the direct presence of God. In fact, during one acid trip, I saw what

I believed was the mind of God. It was a massive, pulsating fireball that seemed to be made of stars and sunsets and everything in the universe that had ever inspired humanity. Paradoxically it simultaneously expanded and condensed into a pyramid that filled the room around me. I was overwhelmed by its intelligence and the unconditional love it radiated.

It was an experience so profound that it should have instantly changed my life. But it didn't. It was just entertainment for me; another far-out drug trip. The next day I was back in the same old rut of reality, going to college, trying to pay bills and dealing with my family. Nothing had changed. My life was still full of obstruction and blockage but after twelve hours of acid-fuelled bliss, it all seemed much harder to handle. To Dr Strassman's disappointment, his subjects, who were administered DMT in a clinical controlled environment, didn't capitalise on the psychological or spiritual breakthroughs that they had experienced either (Strassman 2001, p. 276).

It wasn't until I had given up drugs and taken up spiritual studies and practice that I realised that I didn't 'earn' those blissful LSD experiences. The experience was chemically induced, not internally generated. I hadn't transmuted the obstructions and distortions in my Energy Field through years of disciplined training. I didn't have the physiological, emotional or spiritual grounds to process or integrate what I had been shown. In retrospect, using LSD to launch ourselves into realms totally beyond our comprehension was as outrageous as deciding to participate in a grand prix in my old Kombi. There would be no way either myself or my car would be able to match the sleek custom-built sports cars driven by highly trained professionals and I would never consider doing such a thing. However, I would happily drop acid and hope to meet God.

IMBALANCES CREATED BY PSYCHEDELIC DRUGS

If you regularly use hallucinogens you might appear to be physically healthy—unlike a speed or heroin user—but based on my own experience, I believe that hallucinogens disturb the functioning of the mind and create imbalances in your Energy Field which may take many years to recover from. One acid trip can change you forever. A patient of mine had taken LSD while she was at university and the experience never left her. She had a terrible trip and could never go into the room where it had happened again, because she had seen goblins there.

A couple of months after taking the trip she started having flashbacks, where she would see after-images of objects, or stationary objects sliding back and forth, or trails of moving images and patterns. These flashbacks were accompanied by panic, anxiety and fear. In addition, her husband had told her that she was beginning to say strange things and she was terrified that the LSD had done permanent damage to her brain. She felt guilty for having 'brought it on herself'. She had taken the acid seeking a spiritual experience but felt she had ruined her life.

I believe that psychedelic drugs diminish the potential for productive spiritual experiences. I know many people, mainly ex-hippies, who regularly use hallucinogens such as magic mushrooms in a meditative or spiritual context. After years of use they have learned how to control hallucinogenic states. They create the right environment with music, candles, incense or religious imagery and so on, before taking their substance of choice and then, during onset, use breathing or chanting to prevent a bad trip. For them there is often no distinction between drugs and spiritual experiences but, to me, taking hallucinogens to have spiritual experiences is like smoking dope to become more productive: it creates imbalances that will eventually generate the exact opposite results.

Hallucinogens put you in an extreme state and the more often you take trips the more your balance of Yin and Yang will be affected. This imbalance will affect your life on every level. For example, communicating with others becomes less effective because listening and cognition require strong Yin. Without this, you talk 'at' someone, not 'with' them. I remember a guy I knew who had taken LSD regularly for years. He was in the music industry and had a similar drug history to mine but he had continued using drugs rather than going down the path of repair. I used to meet him for lunch occasionally. It was always slightly frustrating because he didn't seem to listen to anything I said and his responses to what I did say were always slightly irrelevant or off-centred. He didn't have the Yin to allow any real interaction to occur.

Inevitably this inability to communicate will affect your world view and impact upon all your social interactions. Because of the law of attraction, in which 'like attracts like', you will attract extreme situations in your relationships and work, and an edge of madness will pervade your life. But you won't perceive it as such because extreme states will have become your norm. My friend had an ongoing series of intense but short-lived relationships with women. Each time I met him he would describe yet another break-up. This was usually due to an alternating cycle of dramatic fights and excessive sex.

He kept using LSD because he wanted spiritual experiences; he would justify his drug use by claiming that plants that induce hallucinations were traditionally used in shamanic cultures as an integral part of their spiritual life. But taking hallucinogenic substances in those cultures is so far removed from the 'recreational' context in which drugs are used in the West that comparison is fruitless. I also think, based on years of spiritual practice and the study of diverse spiritual luminaries ranging from Yogananda to the Dalai Lama, that just because hallucinogenic substances form part of particular esoteric practices, it doesn't necessarily mean that they serve the higher purpose of spiritual growth.

In terms of their actions on the Human Energy Field, spiritual practices and hallucinogenic drugs are complete opposites. You need an appropriate internal environment to process spiritual experiences. Hallucinogens remove the basis for beneficial spiritual experiences because they separate body, mind and spirit. I believe that the only beneficial way to explore the non-material aspects of our reality is via Chi-training practices such as Tai-chi, Chi-gung or yoga. These are designed to balance Yin and Yang and ultimately unite you with the creative forces that make up the universe. These techniques can guide you step by step beyond the boundaries of reality into other-worldly dimensions. They allow you to expand the boundaries of Yang, or mind, in the presence of Yin, or body, and thus truly expand your consciousness.

CHAPTER FOUR

Speed, heroin and addiction

HIGHER AND LOWER

Towards the end of the forest mescaline trip I had hugged Karl and he had whispered the forbidden word—heroin. He wondered, given the amazing trip we had had on mescaline, what heroin might be like. For days afterwards his words kept echoing around in my head. I felt both attracted and repulsed by the idea of heroin. In hippie circles, it was not a cool drug. It was what you took when you no longer wanted to be actively and passionately engaged in life. On heroin, there was no communication, no loving, caring or sharing. Heroin made people introspective, emotionally cool, silent and still. It represented spiritual defeat.

John Lydon, formerly Johnny Rotten of the Sex Pistols, summed up the attitudes of the time when, in discussing Sid Vicious' 1979 heroin overdose, he stated that 'speed had been the drug of choice in those days not heroin. Heroin was a dirge of self-pity, a stupid, negative drug' (Smith 2004).

I was also worried about how addictive heroin was supposed to be. There was a squat where we occasionally used to score hash that was occupied by a group of heroin addicts. There were piles of rubbish everywhere and there was no electricity or plumbing. The junkies would use the corner of one of the rooms as a toilet. It was a really dark and depressing place but the addicts didn't notice. They were at the stage where they would do anything to get their next fix. The heroin had destroyed their spirit and passion for life. Although it is less than ten percent of users who reach this point of total dependency (Carnwath & Smith 2002, p. 86), we didn't want to end up like that. At the same time though, heroin was the ultimate drug; the way we were going it was really just a matter of time until we tried it.

HEROIN AND MACRAMÉ

After I finished work at the day-care centre, where I was doing the practical component of my college course in social pedagogics, I met Karl, Dietrich and Stefan and we went to score. I had to go back to work that night, in my own time, to demonstrate macramé at a parent–teacher evening. Spending the evening doing craft for some middle-aged straight people was not something I had the slightest interest in so I was hoping to get some speed to motivate me.

We had just discovered speed and I loved the thrilling rush it created, but when we arrived at the dealer's place he only had heroin. Karl and I looked at each other for a moment. We had never followed up on our heroin conversation or even mentioned it again but then neither of us had forgotten it either. The dealer warned us that the heroin was very pure and we should be careful how much we took. Curiosity won out over fear and we decided to buy some.

We went back to Stefan's place. He opened the foil and, to our surprise, we discovered a brown, dirty-looking powder. It was 'brown sugar', a special blend that was suited to smoking. I was glad because at that stage even though Stefan had syringes ready, I was still too scared to inject myself. We decided to 'chase the dragon' or inhale the smoke created by heating the aluminium foil with a cigarette lighter. Stefan went first then Karl, then it was my turn. I felt slightly apprehensive. I inhaled the smoke deeply and slowly.

As soon as the heroin entered my bloodstream I realised that this was a drug in a league of its own. Within minutes, I fell into the most single-minded state I have ever experienced. My vision zoomed in to one spot, allowing my entire consciousness to focus on one detail at a time. It was as if nothing else existed except what I was looking at. My peripheral vision was blanketed in a soft haze of the most beautiful shade of pink I had ever seen. Physically, I felt like I was glued to my seat but I was completely content to be that way. I had no desire to move and no reason to move. Everyone else must have felt the same because no one spoke and no one initiated any kind of activity. We could have been anywhere, it really didn't matter.

After a while I made my way back to work. I was acutely aware of being in a very different state from everyone else. My pupils were like pin-holes and my eyes were shining too brightly. I avoided making eye contact with anyone, as I was sure that if I did they would realise that I was smacked-out. Curiously though I didn't feel any panic, fear or paranoia about it. I was utterly calm and centred.

When I arrived, the director of the centre was still address-
ing the parents so I took a seat at the back of the room and
focused on being quiet and still. After he finished I went into
my classroom to do my macramé demonstration. I had a half-
finished pot-hanger already prepared, as my plan had been to
focus on showing the details of the knotting. Thanks to the
heroin I was now in good shape for details. I picked up the
strings. I could sense the group of people watching me but
everything around me seemed to be happening in slow
motion. The only thing that existed for me was the pot-hanger
directly in front of my eyes. In a state of total concentration
I carefully folded one string over the other. I became totally
immersed in the process of making the knots.

The next morning I fronted up to work, straight and clear-
headed again. I was sure that someone would have realised that
I had been on drugs. Sure enough, ten minutes later I got called
into the head office. With a feeling of dread I went in; I knew
that this was the end. The director had probably received com-
plaints from the parents and I would be thrown out of the
centre and probably college as well. I was already in enough
trouble with my family for taking drugs, this would be the final
straw.

Instead, I was met with a beaming smile and congratulations
for presenting an outstanding demonstration. Apparently the
parents were impressed by my performance and the commitment I had shown towards the craft. Some said that I was an
example of how easy it was to be misled by appearances.
Because I had long hair and dressed like a hippie they had
assumed that I would be a sullen, disinterested drug-user.
Instead I showed confidence, focus and dedication; qualities
that most of my generation lacked. He thanked me for creating
a good impression for the centre and asked me to keep up the
good work.

DECLINE AND FALL

A year later everything changed. One of my lecturers had spoken to me in private about drugs. She pretended to be interested in trying them herself and wanted to know what it was like. Believing she was genuine I described some of my drug experiences but she immediately reported our conversations back to Herr Schmidt, the college director. The following day I got called into his office and before I even had a chance to speak, he said that he had heard that I was a drug-user and he informed me in a dictatorial tone that this revealed anti-social behaviour and poor leadership skills. To show my 'commitment to change' and to prove my 'loyalty to the country', I should voluntarily do two years in the army. After that he would consider allowing me to come back and start the course again from the beginning. The two years of study that I had already completed were now worth nothing.

If I didn't do what he said, I would be thrown out of college immediately. Paperwork would be issued documenting the fact that I had ceased studying and was now eligible for national service. Either way I was going to end up in the army. I felt desperate and trapped. I knew that military service would mean the end of my dreams. The army specialised in breaking people like me. Friends of mine who had been pacifists but had been forced to do their national service had never been the same afterwards. I could have gone to court to contest service on the grounds that I was a pacifist, but the word was that the judges were all ex-Nazis with no empathy for 'weak pacifists'. Germany in those days was a conservative and controlled society with no place for non-conformists of any kind. Drug-users were considered dirty and criminal by mainstream society and the hippie revolution had made no inroads into that attitude.

Even my family, who were relatively open-minded, had forced me to see a counsellor about my drug use, as if it was a serious problem. Like the lecturer at college who had set me up and turned me in, the counsellor had first pretended to be sympathetic and interested in drugs. He said he had travelled in Afghanistan and had been a hippie himself. He asked to see my stash. I showed him my block of hash and told him how LSD expanded consciousness and showed us our potential. He then flushed the hash down the toilet and jeered at me in front of his colleagues. He told me that the idea of expanding one's consciousness was crap and that if I wanted entertainment, I should just get drunk like every-body else. It was a humiliating experience and the worst thing he could have done. It made me feel even more alien-ated from society and more drawn to drugs.

Like the two-faced counsellor, Director Schmidt epito-mised the worst of the country. He looked like a Bavarian farmer with his ill-fitting suit, crew-cut grey hair and boiled pink skin. I had to throw away two years of study and then join the army and waste another two years of my life simply because he said so. The injustice of it all welled up in me; they were all the same: the teachers, the police and the politicians. My pent-up anger and frustration with the way I had been betrayed and let down by the whole smug, cor-rupt society erupted. I screamed 'fuck off' at him and stormed out the door, slamming it after me.

Going underground

In that moment my life changed. Now if I didn't do my national service I would be considered a deserter and once the military police found me they would forcibly take me off to the barracks. My only option was to go underground so they couldn't find me. This meant that I could have no official identity, so I couldn't work or study. It was the beginning of the end for me. I hung around in abandoned buildings with my friends who had also deserted or run foul of the law. We moved into the shadow side of society.

There were no assignments, no rules and no regulations in my life now, but instead of enjoying that freedom I began to feel disillusioned. There was no reason to get up each day. I took more LSD, to try to recapture my passion for the hippie dream and expanded consciousness but it didn't work. Bizarrely, I found myself envying people who had a normal life; who went to work every day and could look forward to their weekends. I desperately needed some focus or direction in my life again. But I couldn't change my external reality even if I had wanted to, because whatever I did I would just end up in the army or in jail as a deserter, so I would have to change my internal world instead and at that time drugs were my only way of doing that.

Giving up drugs was simply out of the question. I still believed that they were the only way of accessing that fantastic state that my first joint had shown me and a life without that was empty. I couldn't relate to people who were not chasing that state. Marijuana and hash couldn't take me there any longer and the more LSD I took the more scary it became because the trips were getting really bad. Heroin was not an option—it was too numbing, so I turned to cocaine.

COCAINE

Cocaine, a natural stimulant obtained from the leaves of the coca plant, was first isolated in the West in the 19th century and immediately hailed as a miracle drug. It was widely prescribed and freely available until the early 20th century when its side effects began to be understood. Following an epidemic of abuse it was banned, but made an illicit comeback in the late 1960s, coincidentally at the time that speed temporarily fell from favour (Booth 2003, p. 313). Cocaine use peaked in the early 80s, when it was estimated that over 10 million people in the USA alone tried it. In 2003, world production was estimated at 655 tons (UNODC 2004). Its recent annual worldwide sales are estimated to generate 92 billion US dollars—more than McDonald's, Microsoft and Kellogg's combined (Streatfeild 2001). In the 1961 UN Convention on Narcotic Drugs, cocaine was classified as having addictive properties and presenting a risk for abuse although preparations of cocaine are accepted as having medical value.

Cocaine had an air of mysticism and ritual associated with it. I loved the accoutrements involved in taking it, the mirrors and small spoons, but I also loved the way it motivated us all again. Cocaine was a creative drug. If we snorted it we could have long and passionate philosophical discussions, like we used to have in the old days on marijuana or hash. Cocaine was reminiscent of mescaline too in the warmth it generated, and it had a sacred feel. I would have taken it all day every day but it was really expensive and often unavailable for months at a time so we started using more speed.

Speed too made life feel exciting again. It mightn't have had the same 'warmth' as cocaine, but it was freely available at a fraction of the cost. Speed also made everything feel meaningful and structured. It put a sense of purpose into my aimless life. It was great.

SPEED

'Speed', or methamphetamine, is now the most commonly abused illicit drug after cannabis. It is a derivative of amphetamine, a synthetic stimulant which emerged in the 1920s and was widely prescribed in the 1950s and 60s as a treatment for depression and obesity. The 1971 UN Convention on Psychotropic Substances classified methamphetamine as presenting a risk for abuse and posing a serious threat to public health but, unlike drugs such as heroin and marijuana, it was also considered to have some therapeutic value. However, the UNODC (United Nations Office on Drugs and Crime) has recently identified amphetamine-type stimulants (ATS), as erroneously perceived to be less harmful than substances such as heroin and cocaine, and also noted increasing consumption, which in South-East Asia is turning into an alarming epidemic. The dramatic increase in the worldwide seizure of illegal laboratories— from 1000 in 1995 to over 10 000 in 2002—is some indication of the escalating production and use of ATS drugs (UNODC 2004).

HIGH ON SPEED

Powerful stimulants like speed or cocaine intensify mental and physical experiences because they make the organs function at peak level. On speed you feel invincible. Not surprisingly, during World War II Japan, Germany and the USA provided the drug to their armies to increase endurance and stamina (Anglin et al. 2000). But speed does much more than that: it can make you feel that you are spiritually, emotionally and physically perfect, a 'master of the universe' (UNODC 2004). But those feelings are not real; they are drug induced. However, they could be real. Drugs like speed or cocaine can provide a glimpse of how good you could feel naturally, or even perhaps how humans are truly destined to feel.

Natural vs Unnatural highs

Spiritual masters, leaders and gurus devote their whole lives to achieving that kind of perfect state without drugs. Regardless of which practice they follow, Taoist, Buddhist, Hindu etc., they all describe achieving similar states of bliss, of vibrating with euphoria. They feel invincible. One spiritual leader I met even described it as being in a permanent state of orgasm. But they feel like this because they have mastered physical reality by balancing Yin and Yang and by regulating the flow of Chi. They know how to control and nurture the elements. They have built Blood, Chi and Jing through disciplined daily practice, correct action and appropriate diet. Combined with their commitment to attain perfection, they have created an organ condition and Energy Field capable of experiencing bliss and euphoria on a permanent basis.

Using speed or cocaine to generate bliss or euphoria is the opposite process. Rather than feeling great as a result of a strong inner energy, these drugs get you high by exploiting your inner energy, your Jing, which eventually makes you feel really bad.

SPEED INTERPRETED USING TRADITIONAL CHINESE MEDICINE

Because speed draws energy from Jing rather than from nutritional food and drink that has been converted via the Stomach and Spleen into energy, there is no hunger stimulus (this is why amphetamines are used in many diet drugs) and regular speed-users rarely eat. This accelerates the development of serious side effects. Because Jing is being depleted, the body needs nutrient-rich food and drink more than ever, but as the signal to eat is bypassed, more Jing is exploited. Jing is supposed to be treasured and conserved as it is either difficult or impossible to replenish, depending on what school of thought you subscribe to. But getting high on speed wastes your Jing and accordingly shortens your life.

Mainlining, or injecting, speed accelerates the ageing process even more. In the 1960s, when it became common knowledge that injecting rather than swallowing amphetamines led to a far more intense hit (Streatfeild 2001, p. 210), intravenous amphetamine abuse spread among a subculture known as 'speed freaks'. This practice led to many teen mortalities. American coroners of the time were baffled by the deaths of these teenagers who were theoretically in the prime of their lives but the subsequent autopsies revealed young bodies with the internal organs of eighty-year-olds (Streatfeild 2001, p. 210).

Spleen Chi deficiency

The Spleen, which produces Chi and Blood, is the major organ adversely affected by speed, and after a period of speed use it develops a condition called Spleen Chi deficiency. This means that all functions of the Spleen will be lessened. The Spleen influences the capacity to think, concentrate and focus and it also processes and 'transports' thought and emotionality. As its function deteriorates thoughts will no longer be transported smoothly. The Spleen is also associated with the Earth element which enables the establishment of healthy boundaries and forms the basis for sound ego development. With Spleen Chi deficiency and depleted Earth energies, not only can you no longer communicate effectively but the process of cognition becomes inhibited and the idea of 'self' becomes hard to grasp; just as you can't grasp a complex mental concept when you are exhausted.

Earth energies provide reference to centre; as they decline you start to feel that your centre has been shifted outside of yourself. Then you begin to perceive this displacement as someone else standing behind you. This triggers the classic speed or cocaine-fuelled paranoid belief that you are constantly being followed. I remember seeing a major rock star interviewed on television in the 1970s. It was filmed in an empty studio but during the interview he kept looking behind him and occasionally he asked the interviewer if there was someone there. The interviewer was unnerved by this behaviour and had no idea what was going on. But the rock star had the drawn-in cheeks, thin body and characteristic pallor of long-term cocaine or speed use.

Blood deficiency

Most heavy speed-users become pale because they develop a condition which is called 'Blood deficiency' in Traditional Chinese Medicine. This is not the kind of condition that would show up in a Western blood test as, in TCM, 'Blood' is an entirely different concept. It is considered a dense and material form of Chi (Maciocia 1989, p. 48), so Blood deficiency is a kind of vital force deficiency.

Trying to operate on deficient Blood is like trying to run a car on low-grade fuel. All the engine parts will be under stress and nothing will work properly.

Continuing to take stimulants like speed or cocaine after developing Blood deficiency seriously affects the Heart as well. Stimulants force the Heart to work hard but the deficient Blood is unable to provide the nutrients and Chi necessary to support this action so the Heart can suffer not only physiologically, as in the case of drug-related heart attacks, but also emotionally. In TCM, the Heart supports the mind, so as the functions of the Heart become affected, the pathologies of the Heart and mind—mental restlessness, depression, anxiety and insomnia—will arise.

LOSING THE PLOT

My speed use eventually delivered those symptoms. I was thin, white, constantly fatigued and often convinced that people were following me or talking about me. Communicating with people had become a problem as well. I would know what I wanted to say but when I started to speak my mind would suddenly feel like a void: a threatening, blank space. I'd lose the thread of what I was talking about and then say something that had no relevance to the topic or conversation.

I remember being at my parents' place for breakfast one Sunday morning after a night of heavy speed and alcohol abuse. The family were all sitting around the table and I was halfway through a sentence when the void hit me. There was an extremely uncomfortable silence as everyone waited for me to finish what I was saying but the harder I tried to remember what it was, the more it eluded me. In desperation I forced myself to keep talking to try to ground myself, but I found myself suddenly talking about something completely unrelated. Everyone stared at me blankly. I had no idea what I was saying. To escape the intense physical and psychological discomfort I got up and walked out, pretending I had something to do. I kept walking until a sense of centre came back.

The more speed I took, the more often the void hit. People started to look at me as if I was weird and eventually I became anxious about every interaction, particularly if there was a group of people involved. I started to wear a wide-brimmed hat to prevent eye contact with anyone. These days I would probably be wearing a beanie pulled low over my eyes and a hood to limit my visual contact with others and thus preserve some sense of identity.

Without speed I had no sense of centre and I felt scattered, anxious, off-grounded, dizzy and shaky in the limbs. I also had the frequent sensation of imminent fainting. The only thing that could make these symptoms go away was more speed or amphetamine, but each time I came down

I felt worse. Everything in the real world annoyed me. The way people looked, the way the walls looked, the way the furniture looked, the way doors opened and closed, it all made me want to cry or scream. All of us felt the same and to keep these side effects at bay we started 'topping ourselves up' every three or four hours. Otherwise life was depressing and unbearable.

NEEDING SPEED

By 10:00 a.m. I was hanging-out for speed so I went to the market place to score and to my surprise found Stefan there. He had just been released from jail that morning. The police had raided our last squat and found a kilo of hashish and a few grams of speed. Stefan was the only one there at the time. He had refused to name anyone else involved with the drugs and he got arrested and thrown in jail. I was shocked by his appearance. He had been the most passionate of all of us but now his prison-short hair revealed dark and empty eyes and he looked defeated. There was no spark between us when we met. We had been best friends, we had explored other dimensions together, but now we could barely talk to each other.

He must have sensed the state I was in because he silently handed me five prescription amphetamines in tablet form and a bottle of beer. Legality and illegality were concepts that were no longer of any real concern to us. I would often get prescription drugs from a doctor I knew who was himself addicted to painkillers. I swallowed the pills and washed them down with the beer. As the drugs began to dissolve in my stomach the familiar sensation of amphetamines surfaced on my tongue. My anxiety vanished and I could understand my feelings and connect them to actions and words. Everything began to make sense again.

We wandered over to a Gluhwein (mulled wine) stand and ordered some of the hot spiced wine. We stood there happily observing the external world that we were now part of. An old man sitting next to me asked for the mustard. I passed it across, looked into his eyes and chatted to him, radiating confidence and self-assurance. I felt connected to him and could see that he too was pleased by our interaction. He obviously thought I was normal and capable of normal communication.

Being temporarily perceived as 'normal' was such a thrill for me that I savoured the experience for hours afterwards. I went back to the squat, rolled a joint and lay back on a mattress on the floor. The pills allowed the dope to work positively and, as I smoked, I replayed every moment of the brief conversation over and over again in my head. Before long I was checking my watch though. The pills would wear off soon and I automatically started to think about how I could get more of them or some speed. I wanted to stay in that 'drug-normal' state. I couldn't bear the idea of coming down again. Life without drugs was torture.

PARANOIA, DRUGS AND VIOLENCE

As we took more speed, sickness became a major part of our lives. Our old motto of 'make love not war' turned into the cold-hearted expression of advanced Earth energy distortions: 'if you want to vomit, you'd better eat'. Now I knew that something was fundamentally wrong with me. I didn't want to be the only one so screwed-up though, so I desperately looked for evidence of psychological disorders in other people. Then I didn't feel so alone. If I came into contact with people who seemed happy and normal I would try and trigger discomfort, anger or unease in them, then I was in my comfort zone. Then I could relate to them.

This is not only the behaviour pattern of a speed-user of course, anyone who has serious organ imbalances that manifest emotionally and mentally may act in a similar manner. They can't help but aggravate, annoy or accuse you until they can make you react emotionally: it's as if they need to get you in a similar emotional state to them so that they can somehow relax. In the end though, it just makes people want to avoid their company.

Our long-term speed and amphetamine use ended up creating a combination of Blood deficiency, Spleen Chi deficiency, Earth energy depletion and Heart imbalances. This generated an intense agitation and anger in us. Instead of being pacifists we became reactive 'activists'. We were angry with the society that had rejected us, with the people who had betrayed us and with the way our lives had turned out. We could only see what was wrong with everything. When these feelings got to the stage where they could no longer be suppressed, we turned on society.

At that time Germany was at the height of the most terrifying era since the Second World War. A generation of young Germans were desperate to absolve themselves of the national guilt they felt they had unjustly inherited, and supporting terrorist activities against the symbols of the German establishment seemed like the way. Scores of terrorist groups were active and there were constant bomb-blasts, political demonstrations and street battles with the police. We would join in regardless of the cause, screaming abuse and battling the armies of police.

In the midst of all this violence we discovered a surprising sensation of harmony. This was because our external environment now perfectly reflected our internal state. From then on anger, anarchy and violence became part of our world. We began to dress in the aggressive style of the punk movement and replaced our peace signs with the anarchists' symbol. We started creating our own incidents, roaming the streets and shouting outside police stations. The scale of these incidents slowly escalated and after several months became larger and more organised. It wasn't long before we were wearing scarfs to protect us from tear-gas and carrying tennis-rackets to hit back the gas bombs thrown by the police.

Emboldened by our power, a large group of us decided to storm and occupy an old apartment building which was empty and about to be demolished. For one long week police circled the building day and night. Secretly, we were terrified that at any minute they would burst in, beat us all and drag us off to jail. This was the usual process in Germany. But nothing happened. We had unwittingly stumbled onto some council corruption and the police remained outside the building, obviously hoping that we would become demoralised and leave. That way there would be no political fallout. The building had historical value and the last thing anyone wanted was attention drawn to the plans to demolish it.

The press started covering the situation and then the public rallied behind us thinking that we were trying to save the building. I became the spokesperson for the group and found myself meeting with the Mayor and the council demanding to be legally allowed to occupy the building. We never got an official response from them but they didn't throw us out either. Living standards were rough but we were temporarily uplifted and unified by a cause. We got a printing press and began to design and produce radical leaflets, which we distributed to the community.

Homemade banners with all sorts of slogans hung down from most of the windows of the building and hardly a day went by when my face or the antics of our group did not appear in the local newspaper. The police finally left and soon it became a no-man's-land, a lawless enclave. Eventually the euphoria of political activism wore off and the drugs and the circumstances weakened our spirits again. Organised crime infiltrated our ranks and people began using the premises to store drugs. There were endless arguments and fights. Graffiti appeared on every wall. It became a dangerous place to be even for the occupants. Many people armed themselves with knives for their own protection.

By then my dreams were gone and my life had become nothing more than pain and violence. I felt sick and I looked sick. I had sunken cheeks and black holes for eyes. My gaze was expressionless. I was so far gone I took pride in the way I looked, in the evidence of my physical destruction. Speed was the only thing left that gave my existence meaning so I sat back, took my speed and detached myself from the world. My own purpose and destiny were no longer relevant.

I medicated myself into oblivion until a visit from a representative of a serious terrorist organisation shocked me out of my apathy. Apparently they had been keeping an eye on us and had seen some anarchic potential in our situation. Hardline terrorist tactics were suggested and bombs were mentioned. Initially I just couldn't grasp that the conversation was even happening. A few words from this man, with his cold, fanatic's eyes, blew away the last shreds of my hippie visions of a society built on peace, love and harmony. How could he possibly believe I was like him. What had I become?

Horrified I ran out of the building and drove to the forest. I left the car and walked to a spot surrounded by huge old trees that had been my favourite place during my happy hippie drug days. I collapsed on the ground. Reality hit. I was a physical, spiritual and emotional wreck. An outcast and criminal, loathed by society. I had no future and nothing left to live for. It was all over. I sat there and cried for hours. I decided that when the army found me, as they inevitably would, I would simply end it all. I'd overdose or jump from a bridge. I felt so empty inside that death now seemed easier than living.

HEROIN AND THE GATEWAY CYCLE

When I reached this point, I could have easily taken the next step in the gateway drug cycle which would have been to remove all my pain, fear and guilt with a better drug, but the only drug that can override that degree of organ dysfunction is heroin. Heroin is a totally Yin drug. It centres you and cocoons you from the harshness of reality. On heroin I could have stayed in the squat and continued to fool myself into thinking that I was doing something meaningful with my life. However, fate intervened and I left Germany and started the long hard road to recovery. I'll never know what would have happened had I stayed.

☯ CASE STUDY: MARIJUANA TO SPEED TO HEROIN

Scotty, the patient who had been suffering from Liver Yin excess states when he used marijuana, headed down the same marijuana to speed path that I did. When he reached the stage of extreme physical and psychological discomfort though, unlike me, he did turn to heroin. The minute he tried it his sense of centre returned and he felt solid and real again. He felt like himself again. On heroin his self-esteem also returned and he could interact with people confidently and effectively. His paranoia and fear vanished and everything he did created an overwhelming experience of union and contentment. The world was his oyster and everything was extremely satisfying. After the torment of speed, only one word can describe this state—bliss.

HEROIN

Heroin belongs to the opiate family. It is derived from morphine, the principal active ingredient of opium. Discovered in 1874 and marketed commercially in 1898 as a treatment for tuberculosis, heroin was thought to be non-addictive and also useful as a cure for respiratory illness or morphine addiction as it relieved withdrawal symptoms. Later it was discovered to be just as addictive as morphine (Carnwath & Smith 2002 pp. 16–19) but by then illicit markets had been established. The UN Convention of 1961 classified heroin along with cannabis as Schedule IV drugs—those considered to be the most dangerous of the narcotic substances, with high potential for addiction and extremely limited medical value. Treatment data consistently shows that, of the illicit drugs, heroin has the most severe consequences for the user. In 2003 global potential heroin production was estimated at 480 tons (UNODC 2004). Myanmar, Laos and Afghanistan are the primary cultivators of illicit opium poppy and the Afghan crop alone is estimated to be worth 28 billion US dollars (Parenti 2005).

Heroin feels so good that, despite its dangers, it quickly becomes a necessity. Heroin is a lifestyle, and as long as you stay on it, it will allow you to be who you want to be. Unfortunately, within a few months of daily use, it takes over the management of the body, mind and spirit and it controls your decision making and behaviour. Free choice is gone and you get caught in the slow and gradually tightening grip of addiction. You find yourself on a lonely journey in which all social rules become meaningless and everything revolves around heroin.

Now, the signs and symptoms of its true destructive nature are revealed and a desperate battle begins to suppress the horrifying realisation that you have handed your life over to a drug. You don't live for yourself anymore, you live for the synthetic correction of constantly increasing imbalances and dysfunctions. It becomes a full-time commitment just to monitor your wellbeing. There seems to be no way to turn back. If you stop taking the drug, the result is unbearably intense pain. Symptoms escalate and you keep increasing the dose, but after a while what used to deliver a fantastic high now merely corrects the imbalances. Life becomes black and white. All your energy is focused on trying to stay one step ahead of the pain. Nothing else matters.

HEROIN INTERPRETED USING TRADITIONAL CHINESE MEDICINE

Heroin primarily targets the Kidneys which store the Jing. The Kidneys are also the foundation of the Yin and Yang of every other organ. So heroin can artificially correct all organ Yin and Yang imbalances. It can generate freeflow and remove pain of any sort when no other drug can. This is why it is the ultimate drug in the gateway cycle.

However, heroin is also the most devastating drug because it affects the very core of your existence. It rapidly depletes the Jing and also affects the Water element, which is considered to be the carrier of life force. The resultant loss of Jing and weakening of the Kidneys and Water element accelerates ageing and creates physical changes that make heroin addicts look older than they are. Their hair becomes thin, grey and dull. Their teeth turn black and become loose; a problem most people mistakenly think is due to a lack of hygiene. Their skin becomes pale and scaly with dark spots, another exterior symptom of severe Jing depletion which can easily be mistaken for a lack of hygiene.

After a period of heroin addiction, bones become brittle and break easily. Fatigue, loss of libido and depression are the norm, and constant weight loss occurs. Memory fails, willpower and motivation decline, fears arise and phobias take over. Eventually you are so depleted that life becomes nothing more than chronic pathology and you virtually wither away.

In order to get a high, you need healthy organs. But once you get to an advanced stage of heroin addiction, the organs can no longer create enough Chi and Blood to provide you with a high as you have over-exploited your Jing. You need to keep taking more and more heroin of better and better quality to feel anything. Eventually you become so tolerant to it that you are constantly in danger of overdosing. I have seen people adding all kinds of crazy things to heroin in a desperate attempt to get a rush, but due to organ deterioration, imbalances and depletion of Jing, there is simply nothing left to base feelings on. After heroin there is no better drug left either, so at this point the choices are death or change.

MAKING YOUR DRUG PAST AN ASSET

When Scotty became a heroin addict he lost his job and he began lying and stealing from friends and family to support his habit. Eventually he overdosed and was taken to hospital. After that his parents forced him into a rehabilitation program that focused on making him admit guilt and feel bad for taking drugs. He managed to recover and stay clean but he constantly felt as if something was missing from his life. When he came to see me he was hesitant about mentioning his drug past as he was expecting more condemnation. However, when patients present conditions related to drug use, I always start by acknowledging that drug highs are an enjoyable and exciting experience. Drugs make you feel good and we all want that.

On a deeper level, the state that the drugs evoke can make you feel love or make you feel accepted, so by taking drugs you may have subconsciously been trying to meet the needs of your soul. It is not a crime or a sickness to desire these things and I firmly believe that people are not bad for taking drugs. This attitude just creates negative thought patterns in the user. My own drug use generated so much abuse from people that 'addict', 'loser', 'hopeless' and 'fucked-up' were the words left permanently floating in my head. Shame and guilt settled down deep into my psyche. This was really not helpful to me and it made the recovery process that much harder.

As I explained to Scotty, your past can be an asset regardless of how it was spent. Every experience is meaningful as long as you learn something from it. The negative outcomes of drug use, the physical, psychological and spiritual damage, need to be addressed, as does the wider social damage. At the same time though, a crucial part of the repair process is to work on recapturing the fantastic freeflow states that drugs can generate, but to create them in a beneficial manner. Otherwise your life will feel somehow empty.

I devised a full recovery program for Scotty and he embraced a lifestyle based on getting healthy highs. He then came to realise that his experiences on the frontiers of extreme pleasure and pain, and of a world beyond the imagination of most people, had created a wealth of insight into fundamental universal laws. Accordingly, he was able to understand better than most that to live in accord with these laws rather than in defiance of them is the only way to achieve lasting happiness and health and to be the person he always wanted to be.

CHAPTER FIVE

Ecstasy

THE HIPPIE LEGACY

At the height of our hippie days, we really believed that psychedelic drugs were going to change the world. We thought they would allow everyone to break through limiting thought patterns and set themselves free. But none of us really knew what we were supposed to do with that freedom once we had it and, in the end, our dreams collapsed around us, just as every dream that relies on drugs to manifest itself will.

I think that illicit drugs have a self-sabotaging nature: they will eventually deliver exactly the opposite to what the user intended, and this can apply both on a personal scale and on a larger scale. In regards to the latter, instead of creating a world based on love and peace, the hippie embracement of drugs indirectly spawned the current multi-billion dollar drug industry, which is proving to be socially and spiritually destructive beyond belief.

GLOBAL DRUG STATISTICS

The United Nations Office on Drugs and Crime (UNDOC) 2004 World Drug Report estimates that there were 150 million people using cannabis, 30 million using speed or amphetamines, 8 million using ecstasy, over 13 million using cocaine and 15 million using opiates (heroin, morphine, opium, synthetic opiates), including 9 million using heroin. However, they also note the difficulties in accurately recording illegal use of narcotic and psychotropic substances as it is largely a clandestine sector where information is by definition difficult to obtain. In 2002 across all drug categories nearly 26 billion 'unit equivalents'—a dose enough to give a high—were seized. Ten times this at least possibly remained in circulation—260 billion highs. Street surveys generally indicate an even higher level of illicit drug use.

Of course the hippie movement did have a more beneficial legacy as well. Its philosophy of peace, love and spirituality inspired the New Age movement. This, in turn, triggered the 'wellness industry' which is also developing into a multi-billion dollar business. So we now have a historically unprecedented cultural environment in which the dual hippie interests of drugs and spirituality are both gaining mainstream acceptance. From a therapeutic perspective this is an interesting phenomenon. I believe that drugs can act as a catalyst for personal and spiritual development by providing insight into the fantastic experience of freeflow, which is our birthright, and by creating pain, which is the precursor to change. So, as more and more people take drugs and are then driven to seek change or improvement in themselves, the booming wellness industry is able to cater to their needs holistically.

THE ECSTASY PHENOMENON

However, the concurrent rise of drugs and spirituality has also inspired a massive new wave of drug-takers for whom drugs and spirituality are linked in a very different way. These are second generation users, born of the hippie era and reaching maturity in a culture in which spirituality and drugs have been commodified to the extent that supermodels design couture yoga clothes, TV advertisements for snack food feature characters dressed as Indian holy men, and soft drink ads look like acid trips.

This new drug demographic inherited the environmental concerns and metaphysical yearnings of the hippie movement, but they also acquired an element of the urban interest in hard drugs spawned by the eighties and its anarchic, nihilistic cultural movements such as punk. Their drug of choice, ecstasy, captures elements of both worlds; it blends the softness, sacredness and warmth of a drug like mescaline with the excitement and action of a drug like speed.

ECSTASY

Methylenedioxynmethylamphetamine (MDMA), later termed 'ecstasy', was synthesised in a laboratory in the early 1900s. Its chemical structure bears similarities to both the stimulant methamphetamine and the hallucinogen mescaline. In the 1940s MDMA was tested as an appetite suppressant and then as a potential treatment for Parkinson's disease but due to side effects it was never marketed for either. In the 1950s the CIA and US army tested it but it was found to have no value as a 'psychological' weapon either (Thomas 2002, p. 86). MDMA was listed as a Schedule 1 drug (strictly controlled and having little or no medical use) in the 1971 UN Convention on Psychotropic Substances. Despite this, in the 1970s, primarily due to the work of the chemist Alexander Shulgin, who referred to it as 'penicillin for the soul', MDMA found a largely unapproved use in psychotherapy (Thomas 2002, pp. 84–96). As knowledge of its psychotropic effects widened so did its recreational use. Annual production is now estimated at 113 tons and use continues to increase (UNODC 2004). In 2001 Australia reported the highest levels of ecstasy abuse worldwide (UNODC 2003) and recent Australian surveys suggest that first time and occasional ecstasy users often become habitual users (AIHW 2003).

On one level, I think the recent boom in ecstasy use is connected to a desire for ritual, ceremony and the renewal of interest in spiritual experiences. I have seen a new consciousness rising, particularly in young people, which is driven by the need for belief in a higher power. In his seminal book on

spirituality, Roger Walsh identifies four claims that consti-
tute the core of all religious or spiritual wisdom as follows:
that there are two realms of reality, the physical realm and
the realm of spirit; that humans partake of both realms; that
we can recognise our divine spark; and that realising our
spiritual nature is our highest goal (Walsh 1999, pp. 7–8).
A drug like ecstasy can appear to give instant access to all
this. Unsurprisingly, raves, dance parties and clubs have
almost become the new churches, where ecstasy and the
relentless beat of dance/trance music can deliver euphoric
or sacred experiences on demand. Even though I would
never take a drug again, I can understand the attraction of
belonging to such a rich subculture of spirituality, tech-
nology and music.

My patients' and students' reports of their ecstasy use
identify effects including feelings of insight, empathy and
forgiveness. Some claim to have 'found themselves' or to have
been profoundly changed for the better after taking the drug.
Ecstasy belongs to a category of drugs called entactogens—
meaning literally 'touching within' (Resnick 2001). It was
widely used in USA and is still used in Switzerland as a psychotherapeutic drug in marriage and relationship counselling
(Thomas 2002, p. 93). In the recreational context as well,
ecstasy users identify effects including feelings of insight,
empathy and forgiveness. In light of this, the current boom in
ecstasy use could also be viewed as mass 'self-prescription' of
a drug which can generate loving and spiritual experiences as
well as promoting insight into the self. As a therapist, I think
that desiring insight and love is a positive goal, but using
ecstasy will eventually prevent you from achieving it.

Another reason ecstasy is so popular is that it has the
ability to deliver a glimpse of the breathtaking euphoria we

were chasing with heavy-duty psychedelic drugs like LSD, but because it is milder and also produces stimulant effects, it is simultaneously able to control your mood to a certain degree (presuming it is relatively pure). This means that you are more likely to have a positive experience and less likely to spend hours being harassed by nasty reptiles or aliens. In drug culture this is a good thing. The fact that most ecstasy users are young, in the 14-25 year-old bracket (UNODC 2003) and, according to some sources, getting younger, is also a factor to take into consideration in the drug's popularity, as the organs of young people are more likely to be healthy and functioning well, vastly increasing the possibility of enjoyable drug experiences.

ECSTASY INTERPRETED USING TRADITIONAL CHINESE MEDICINE

If you use the model of Traditional Chinese Medicine to examine its effects, ecstasy could be said to target the Heart and the Spleen. The Heart is the organ responsible for excitement, joy and love, and it also houses the mind. The Spleen is the organ responsible for 'transformation and transportation' and therefore mental clarity. So, when you take ecstasy, the joyful expression of loving thoughts takes top priority. All your deep-seated emotions are transformed and transported by thoughts or actions that have the consistency of liquid. This is why you can communicate with people and behave in a way you couldn't or wouldn't without the drug. Ecstasy shows you how loving, expressive and caring you can be and the dance parties, clubs and raves provide a supportive environment in which to explore this part of yourself.

In a recent publication on ecstasy, the author claimed that the ecstasy/rave scene could be characterised by 'reversion to childhood' (Thomas 2002, p. 44). This was in terms of its fashions, attitudes and accessories such as the dummies or pacifiers that many hard-core ravers carry. According to TCM, the Spleen is also associated with the mouth, with eating, talking, tastebuds and so on. Ecstasy can cause involuntary teeth clenching, grinding or chewing, which I would consider a result of excessive Yang operating in the Stomach meridian. The Stomach is the Yang partner of the Spleen and the upper part of the Stomach meridian runs along the muscles of the mouth. Speed can generate similar symptoms and in my day we would chain-smoke cigarettes to satisfy the need to have the mouth somehow constantly active. Therefore, using a dummy at a rave doesn't really represent regression to childhood; it is primarily to prevent damage to the insides of the mouth.

Nonetheless, on a wider level there is an element of truth to the regression claim due to the imbalances that ecstasy creates in the Earth element, which is associated with the Spleen. Earth element is connected with growth and maturity and, at a fundamental level, with separation from the mother. Hence, children who are considered 'tied to the apron string', who can't separate, can actually be displaying an Earth element weakness. When I was on drugs I was constantly accused of being irresponsible or childish. In hindsight, I probably was behaving in an immature manner because the drugs had affected the Earth element and the normal development of the characteristics of maturity.

Coming down

Although you may initially feel inspired or uplifted by a drug, in the end the higher a drug takes you, the worse you will feel afterwards. Euphoric drug experiences are always followed by the opposite emotional states of emptiness or depression. This is why after an ecstasy weekend many people report feeling really 'off' physically, spiritually and emotionally. This is because the drug has made you feel good by drawing upon your inner energy stores. Afterwards you will be depleted of life-force or fuel and your wellbeing will naturally be affected. It may take days or even weeks for you to catch up again through food and sleep. If you keep taking the drug without allowing yourself to recover, the side effects become worse.

Ideally, after a weekend on ecstasy, you should eat three big nourishing meals a day. Get some extra sleep too. Many people tell me that they want to detoxify themselves after taking drugs, so they go on some sort of 'cleansing diet'. But these diets can be dangerous if the body is already depleted by drugs or other means, as they can deplete you even further. I would never recommend going on drastic diets after any event that has taxed your Jing such as illnesses, accidents, drug trips or childbirth, unless of course you are following professional advice.

Ecstasy and repair

Western medicine, which is based on a division between body and mind, between patient and 'condition', usually lists the possibility of 'brain damage', anxiety, paranoia, irritability, impaired memory function but primarily depression as a result of long-term ecstasy use. In Traditional Chinese Medicine, however, those symptoms, particularly the depression, can be linked to Spleen Chi deficiency and Heart imbalances. Whereas in Western medicine depression is considered to be a 'chemical imbalance' in the brain that can be redressed by administering drugs to 'rebalance' the brain, in TCM psychology and medicine are one, and body, mind and spirit are addressed equally.

Generally speaking, TCM does not view depression as a 'condition' but rather as a symptom, an emotional state arising from underlying imbalances in the organs and Energy Field. In my drug recovery programs I treat post-drug depression through therapy, improved diet, exercise and powerful nutritional supplements to boost organ function. I also include Chi-gung or meditation techniques to cultivate joy. I consider this to be an important component in recovery because of my understanding that any drug use, particularly a drug like ecstasy, is on some level linked to a desire for spiritual experiences. If this is the case and you don't find another means of achieving that state you will never be truly satisfied or happy, and depression can linger.

With the current scale of ecstasy use, post-drug depression may soon become a major health issue. Coincidentally— or perhaps not—the last decade, a period dominated by an increase in the use of ecstasy, has also seen an astronomical rise in the use of antidepressants. But taking one drug to counter the effects of another does not deal with the underlying causes.

ECSTASY AND SPIRITUALITY

I have observed that most students I know who regularly use ecstasy are often also interested in meditative or spiritual practices. For them drugs are easily accessible and spirituality even more so. The general noticeboard at the college where I lecture is plastered with flyers advertising meditation retreats, workshops and seminars run by internationally renowned gurus and spiritual leaders who provide quick access to powerful energetic forces. Many of the students attend one or more of these courses but they also regularly take ecstasy and go to dance parties or clubs. The hours of trance-like dancing and the impression of group bonding generated by the drugs become a quasi-spiritual experience for them and accordingly, in their minds, drugs and spirituality begin to merge.

Their lifestyle, with its free-wheeling mix of recreational drug usage and serious spiritual or meditative practices, is a recent phenomenon. When I was into drugs things were different. We might have been spiritual seekers, but there were no gurus to see or workshops to go to. 'Exotic' religions such as Buddhism were viewed with suspicion and drug users were treated like outcasts and criminals by all but their peers. Unless we went to an ashram in India, getting stoned and listening to Ravi Shankar or wearing Yin and Yang or Om symbols was how we expressed our spirituality. In the 1970s we would pass a black stone 'chillum' (a conical pipe used ritually in India) around and before each of us smoked we used to ceremoniously cry 'boom shanka'. Someone who had been to India told us that that was how it was done there and it banished bad spirits. In those pre-ecstasy days, that, or a good trip, was about as far as the 'drugs and spirituality' combination went.

Now, however, I see scores of young people who have become committed to meditative techniques, Chi-gung or energy channelling such as Reiki but still regularly use ecstasy. For many this has reached the stage where they meditate or even do yoga while waiting for the ecstasy to take effect. However spiritual practices and regular hard drug use don't mix and if you do both for a long period of time it can put such strain on the organs, in particular the Spleen, that it can lead to confusion about reality.

☯ CASE STUDY: COMBINING ECSTASY AND SPIRITUAL PRACTICE

Just such an experience of confusion about reality happened to a young patient of mine, Nick. He spent all day in front of a computer designing games, and evenings in front of his computer and keyboards recording trance music. He was also really interested in spirituality but had never followed up on it. The first time he tried ecstasy he was at a club with some friends of his. He had a fantastic night. The music sounded incredible; it was as if it was playing inside his head and he truly heard it for the first time. He had smoked dope for a few years and thought that it intensified the pleasure of music, but ecstasy took this to another level.

He danced for hours that night and whenever he made eye contact with someone, he felt as if he connected directly with them on a soul level. It was as if there was no longer a filter between him and other people. He felt completely open. His senses, thoughts and feelings revolved around love and he was able to express himself in a deep and emotionally truthful way. For the first time in his life he understood what it meant to open up your heart. On that night, he felt like he understood the teachings of Buddha, the cosmos and the meaning of life. It was all given to him in an instant with one ecstasy pill.

As far as he was concerned ecstasy was a gift from the universe. It allowed human bonding and spiritual fulfilment in a world dominated by shallow materialism, isolation and the fear of strangers. Best of all it was instant. No one in today's world had decades to spend seeking enlightenment through meditation, and with ecstasy you didn't have to; you could get there in twenty minutes. Nick started chasing that state and his ecstasy use gradually increased until, like his friends, he was taking it every weekend. Coming down was a pain in the neck so he tried to limit his intake, but as the raves and the ecstasy highlighted the spiritual significance of his human existence, the material world and material concerns became less important.

One day he saw a poster advertising a charismatic meditation workshop that offered instant access to the super-consciousness via witnessing the ecstatic awakening of the primordial power that lies dormant within.The course claimed to instantly open up all the chakras allowing blissful spiritual fulfilment. It spoke the language of his ecstasy experiences and Nick's attention was instantly captured.He decided to go along to see if it could deliver what it claimed.

The workshop acted as another awakening for him. Within a few minutes of the initiation, a special chant led by the workshop's spiritual leader, Nick was taken into a state of consciousness that he had only known previously through ecstasy and it 'came on' like ecstasy did. Warm currents of love moved through his body and intensified until he needed to physically move to express it. Deep primal rhythms rose up in him and he had flashbacks to what he thought must have been a past life as an Indian warrior. He saw himself being initiated into a sacred rite and then dancing and chanting around a fire. He felt like he was able to bond with the other people in the room in the same soul-connected manner that ecstasy created.

After the workshop he felt a sense of excitement surging through him. He believed that he was now on the real spiritual path. With this new meditative technique, he could access the same state that ecstasy provided but without the unpleasant side effects. He was inspired to become really pure so he stopped using ecstasy and then gave up coffee, alcohol, meat, dairy and eggs in quick succession. He would arrive at work early each morning and would spend fifteen minutes writing spiritual affirmations which he then stuck all over his office partition. He stayed away from his partying friends and went daily to a meditation group.

After a couple of months though, his new lifestyle began to lose its appeal. For some reason the intensity of the meditation was declining and he started to feel a strange sense of emptiness and frustration. He decided this must have been because, even though he was on the right track, socially his life was lacking. The meditation group was now his main form of interaction and, although the people were nice enough, they went to bed early and preferred calming New Age music to dance music. He felt that deep down he wasn't straight like them, and he started to really miss the music and communion of ecstasy-fuelled raves.

He tried to suppress these feelings but after a couple of big weeks at work, gave in and went out with his old friends to a dance party. He took ecstasy and felt fantastic. It was as if he was giving his soul what it had been longing for. He danced for hours with total body–mind connection and interacted with everyone in a loving and caring manner. He decided that an occasional ecstasy experience was okay. But it wasn't long until occasional became regular again and he eventually drifted away from the meditation and back into his old lifestyle.

He felt guilty about using ecstasy regularly again, but life was starting to annoy him and ecstasy could make his annoyance disappear. Coming down each time was getting harder to handle though. He tried to mask the 'off' feelings with marijuana and alcohol but it didn't really work. When he started longing for the weekends so he could take ecstasy again, he knew he had let the situation get out of control. He also knew he could get that state by natural means if he made an effort so he forced himself to stop the ecstasy and go back to the meditation group.

The acceptance and the caring smiles of the people in the group instantly uplifted him. Everyone could smile and be caring on ecstasy, but these people really cared and they didn't need ecstasy to do it. He renewed his commitment to a healthy, spiritual drug-free life. He felt back on track again and he was determined not to lapse. But instead of experiencing the bliss and happiness that this 'spiritual' lifestyle was supposed to be delivering, he found himself feeling ever more frustrated and cynical. Then he developed sleep disturbances and suicidal thoughts began to cross his mind. Eventually he couldn't face the group anymore as the very thought of their friendly, smiley faces annoyed him, so he stopped going.

Now ecstasy was the only way he had to break out of his emotional imprisonment. But because of how he had felt during his 'clean' meditative phases, every time he took ecstasy his mind told him that he was weak, a loser and that he was cheating on his soul. He stopped again and went back to meditation but it couldn't counter his growing feelings of anxiety, fear and depression. So he took ecstasy again. He became firmly trapped in a cycle of two altered states; that generated by the meditation and that generated by the drugs. The intervals between the two decreased, until he got to the stage where he was going to meditation while on ecstasy. Eventually the visions produced by the drugs started to fuse with the experience of the meditation. He began to believe that he was receiving messages from another dimension. Worse still, the messages told him that he was an incarnated soul from a higher plane destined to be a great spiritual leader here on earth.

This had serious repercussions for him in both his private and professional life. He lost his job as he was no longer meeting deadlines and he would often wander around bestowing blessings on his colleagues instead of working. His family and friends had no idea what to do. Most of them didn't want to help anymore anyway because he had become so weird. He was actively projecting his anger and frustration on anyone within reach and was often aggressive and unpleasant. His behaviour scared people or made them feel uncomfortable and they withdrew from him. He couldn't understand why people were avoiding him so he took more drugs to handle it and everything just got worse. He ended up confused and depressed.

Nick was prescribed antidepressants, tranquillisers and sleeping tablets. He had taken the medication but his mother wasn't happy about it. She felt that the underlying cause had yet to be addressed. She had been one of my patients in the past and asked Nick to come and see me. She phoned me first to discuss his situation and see if I could help. I asked her about his symptoms and she said that prior to being treated he was talking disjointedly about what she termed his 'fantasies' such as thinking he knew the Dalai Lama and had an important project to do with him. He was also constantly irritated, frustrated and verbally aggressive. He hadn't used drugs or gone to his meditation group for over eight months now and was behaving in a more rational manner, but he didn't seem like his 'old self'.

Nick came in to see me and we talked at length about his life, his drug use and his interest in spirituality. Even though he appeared subdued, I sensed suppressed frustration and anger. I had seen this before in other patients who regularly mixed drugs and powerful meditative practices. If during deep meditation you unite with the divine source, you receive high energies. In order to be beneficial, these need to be integrated into your life in a productive manner. They should be employed to assist self and others on the journey to spiritual, physical and emotional wellbeing. Taking drugs at the same time prevents you from processing these energies appropriately and you develop organ imbalances which manifest as aggression and anger.

I explained to Nick that I had seen many people who had combined drugs and meditation and that the combination creates energetic imbalances which can generate irritability but also delusions and reactivity. Nick seemed really surprised and perhaps relieved as well that other people had experienced what he had. I told him that meditation targets obstructions in the Energy Field and brings them to the conscious mind. However, because these obstructions are often the result of painful events or incidents that the body has stored to be dealt with at some later stage, when they do come to the attention of the conscious mind, so does the associated emotional pain. This needs to be identified, processed and accepted. It is this that allows the conversion into freeflow and subsequently, finalisation.

When these painful feelings surface, a sense of centre, emotional balance and a strong state of mind are essential to avoid inappropriate reaction. These centred states derive from a healthy balance of Yin and Yang in the organs. Drugs create the exact opposite condition. When you do deep meditation and drugs at the same time, the meditation brings up suppressed and painful memories but due to the drugs you do not have the strength, clarity of mind or the emotional control to process them effectively. In addition, as the primary function of drugs is to suppress physical or emotional pain, each time you stop using drugs all that accumulated pain is released. So you can end up constantly facing emotional and physical pain from both the de-obstruction of the Energy Field and the side effects of the drugs.

The Spleen is the organ that bears the major brunt of this conflict and its deterioration will give rise to the associated Earth energy deficiencies. Then mental imbalances develop, boundaries become unclear and life becomes what we term 'slippery', with a slightly mad flavour attached to everything. Nick said that recently when he woke up he kept thinking about how he had gone to work and blessed people. He couldn't believe that he had acted in such a manner and he was ashamed and embarrassed by what he had done.

I told him that at the time, he would not have had the 'boundaries' that a more balanced person would have. In addition, because Earth energies are also responsible for cognition, if they become deficient it is impossible to have any clarity of vision about what you are doing, so whatever he had done would have seemed perfectly natural. Everyone has done things in the past that they are not comfortable with. But it is through reflecting upon them and accepting them that we learn from them and act differently in the future.

In Bodywork it is accepted that your dominant 'issue' will always surface immediately upon waking, so if he was thinking about it each morning, rather than feeling uncomfortable about what he had done, it was time to grasp that feeling, face it and then accept it. Nick seemed to understand all of this. I told him that my therapy was not about delving into what he had done or not done, but rather about accelerating organ repair so he could regain a sense of centre and well-being which would assist him in accepting and making sense of his past himself.

An important pre-requisite for improving organ function in general and Spleen function in particular is regularity and routine. This means regularly eating warm meals, regular exercise and sleep and so on. However, because most patients with Spleen Chi deficiency, including those whose Spleen Chi has been affected by other causes such as long-term dieting or emotional issues, do not have well established boundaries; their behaviour is usually erratic and emotional. For them regularity or discipline is nearly impossible and they often mock or attack it in others as a way of validating their own behaviour to themselves.

For Nick, I introduced the idea slowly by initially focusing on getting him to have three meals a day at regular times. Once we had that going I added in some morning stretches and then a light program of regular exercise. He still resisted the idea of daily repetition though. But as I explained to him, he already had the skills in place for regularity and repetition. He had been voluntarily seeking and repeating a specific experience and making it a major part of his life with both ecstasy and with meditation. This time though it would be the experience of balanced health he was chasing. The more he did, the more quickly positive emotions would rise again and the easier routine would become for him.

I told him that in my own recovery, just as I had embraced the drug lifestyle and lived in accord with what made me resonate then; the hair, the music, the clothes, the politics and so on, I then embraced the idea of building body, mind and spirit and reinforcing this in every part of my life. Rather than drugs, bongs and Doc Martens, I bought really good running shoes, great hand weights, the best supplements I could get my hands on, meditation CDs, self-help books and clothes and jewellery that would support my new direction. I embraced a whole new culture and lifestyle. I invested in it both emotionally and financially, the way I had done with drugs.

I explained to Nick that his whole ecstasy and meditation period may have been a device to awaken him to a different path. Pain is the most effective medium to instigate long-lasting change and any lengthy period of drug use or other form of extreme or unbalanced behaviour will create physical and emotional pain. The important thing to do then is to see it as an opportunity for positive change.

Once Nick started to view his experiences from this perspective, a significant shift occurred. He stuck to the repair program and also took up Ashtanga yoga, a physically demanding form, and he became stronger and more balanced daily. He realised that the states he had been accessing in an instant manner through charismatic meditative techniques or drugs were much more powerful and fulfilling when they were generated from within and supported by a strong body and mind.

BETTER HIGHS

Nick was not an isolated case. Many people combine ecstasy and meditation or other drugs and spiritual practices. For these people there seems to be a logical connection between the two. I think that there genuinely is a connection. After all, in Western societies it was the widespread use of marijuana in the 1960s that prompted a rise in the study and acceptance of Hindu, Buddhist and Taoist philosophy (Booth 2003, p. 214). This filtered through to mainstream society via the hippie movement and contributed to the current widespread interest in spirituality and self-mastery. In this context the role of drugs was to show glimpses of what we are all really destined for.

Humans are programmed to always go for the better high. It is a fundamental force that drives us forward on every level. If you have developed a taste for fine wines, for example, it is unlikely that you would ever choose to drink poor quality wine again. If you have owned a good car it is difficult to then drive an old bomb. It is the same with drugs and spirituality. Ultimately, the latter delivers much better and more satisfying results. Our body, mind and spirit are destined to operate on a level far superior to anything that drugs can generate and once you head down the path of self-development, you will naturally lose interest in drugs.

What we seek via drugs is already within us. According to Traditional Chinese Medicine, the organs store the secrets of the universe. Each organ not only has a physiological and emotional aspect but also a spiritual aspect, and through managing these we create a spiritually uplifting reality.

CHAPTER SIX

Depression and antidepressants

MOVING TO AUSTRALIA

Shortly after my brush with terrorism in Germany, my parents, for reasons I never really understood, decided to emigrate to Australia. They were buying a property in NSW and wanted me to go to Sydney and act as an interpreter for them with the vendor. I had lived in London for a while as a school student so I was fluent in English, but I think they also realised that I was in serious trouble and this was a way of trying to help me as well. They gave me a ticket to Australia which became, quite literally, my ticket to salvation.

When I arrived in Sydney, it wasn't until I was in the customs queue that I remembered that I had amphetamine pills and hash in my bag. I turned to head for the toilets to get rid of it, but was intercepted by two tanned men wearing long socks and shorts. I had waist-length hair, bare feet and I was still stoned as I had been eating hash and taking tranquillisers on the plane. I must have had 'suspicious' written all over me. The officers took me into a room and searched my bags. When they found the hash they asked me what I was doing with it. I told them I forgot to smoke it before I left. They asked what the pills were and I said I was coming off hard drugs and needed them to stay calm. They looked at me for a moment. Then one of them rolled his eyes, opened the door and casually told me to, 'Fuck off'.

I was shocked at the obscenity and the easy-going tone in which it was delivered. German authorities were arrogant, authoritarian and violent but no one ever swore like that. My first impression was that Australia was a really rude place. On the way out, I asked another customs officer for a good place to go. He looked at me speculatively for a moment and then said, 'Nimbin mate, head north'. I stepped through the door into the brilliant sunshine. Everything looked strange, clean and sharply defined. The sky was a psychedelic-trip blue but the trees seemed to be faded. The heat was intense and some shrill insect noise reverberated through the air. I was a bit disappointed to see the buildings, cars and highways as I had been expecting kangaroos and frontier towns. I had even brought a bush survival knife along with me.

Nimbin

After I had done what my parents wanted, I hitchhiked to Nimbin, which turned out to be a small country town that had become a mecca for dedicated hippies from all over the world. The lush green hills surrounding the town were dotted with communes and alternative homes built of straw or mud-brick. It was what I had longed for in the old days, a community of like-minded people living close to nature in a beautiful setting, but the past two years of speed and anarchy had ruined that dream for me and I no longer knew what I wanted or even who I was.

I had no direction or goals. I couldn't go back to Germany as it would mean going to jail for desertion, so I stayed on in Nimbin. Maybe in a place where no one knew me or reinforced my image of myself as a screwed-up, hopeless addict, things would be different. I tried hard to be normal but my psyche was too shattered to pull it off. On the inside I was so unbalanced I could only relate to what was wrong with people or places. My emotional negativity would inevitably affect whoever I was with, and time and again people would make friends with me but then avoid me when they realised what a psychological mess I was.

Although Nimbin is now swamped with heavy drugs and the scattered, off-centre energy that comes with them, in those days it had a marijuana culture and most people were relatively balanced and grounded. No one was like me. This made me more paranoid about the state I was in. If I had to spend time with people in a confined space, on a car trip for instance, I would take handfuls of over-the-counter codeine tablets, which you would have needed a prescription for in Germany, to numb myself until I was able to pass as nearly normal. In a way I was like a visitor from the future, an indicator of what was to become of Nimbin when the hard drugs came to town, when dealers would peddle speed on the main street and the atmosphere would become much more dark.

In those days though, people grew vegetables and built things and believed in the hippie dream. They would sit around fires in the evening, playing music and passing joints around. I really wanted to be part of that world but I couldn't smoke dope anymore as it was magnifying my imbalances, and I couldn't get speed or other hard drugs. I was effectively being forced to stop using drugs but I had no idea how to interact socially without them. Then I discovered that if I got really drunk first, I could get stoned and be sociable and everyone would think I was a normal, happy, dope-smoking hippie.

Nimbin proved to be the perfect place to start recovering from the physically and psychologically destructive time in Germany. It was a healthy environment to live in then and even though I was drinking lots, without access to hard drugs I slowly became more balanced and centred. I developed an interest in macrobiotics and I even got a job as a cook in the café in town. After about a year my health had improved, my energy had increased and I felt an urge to move into the real world and do something productive.

Living it up

My parents were by then living in the Snowy Mountains, so I decided to join them there. I really wanted professional direction and goals and, as my only recent work experience had been cooking, I decided to continue in that industry. Nimbin had introduced me to the connection between spirituality and vegetarian food and I thought I could now spread the message to a wider audience. I went to the local employment agency and spoke passionately about my vision of peace, harmony and vegetables. I had cut my hair short and worn straight clothes to the interview and, even though I could tell the interviewer was not totally convinced by me, the ski season was about to start and most hotels needed staff.

When I got offered a job as an assistant cook, I eagerly accepted it, keen to start implementing my grand plans. To my disappointment the head chef was not the slightest bit interested in my opinions on anything, let alone vegetarian food. He would throw potatoes at me or turn his radio up when I tried to talk about it. I soon realised that my kitchen skills were not up to speed either. Most of the Nimbin café clientele had been unemployed, so it didn't matter how long you took to cook the meals. If you stuffed up, most people wouldn't even notice as they were usually stoned and anything tastes good when you have the munchies, but the pressure of working in a real commercial kitchen was very different.

It was a bit of a shock to find myself in a world of uniforms, systems and regular work too, and I wasn't sure I had done the right thing by taking the job. By my second week, however, when I discovered that I had landed in the epicentre of a world of raging, drugs, music, sex and skiing, none of that mattered anymore. It was the snow season and the town was full of young people all looking for fun. It was wildly exciting after Nimbin. I started working as a ski instructor as well and whenever I wasn't at work I was skiing or partying with a group of friends. It was the start of the excessive 80s, I was 24 and it wasn't long before I began using speed and cocaine again.

After the snow season ended, I found myself wanting more in the way of work satisfaction. I had spent the last six months preparing prawn cocktails and crumbing schnitzels. My dream to change the world through cooking was not going to happen and I needed another outlet for my idealism and passion.

Recapturing the dream

I went back to the employment office and applied for a job as a project officer on a program which aimed to assist young people obtain jobs by enhancing their creativity, self-esteem and communication skills. I had always wanted to work in a profession that helped people. As a young boy I wanted to be an aid worker in Africa. Then I decided I would be a priest. When I finished school I had started studying social pedagogics, a sort-of cross between social work and education, but because I had been thrown out of college before I had completed my degree, I had never had a chance to work in the field. My new employer thought that the two years of study that I had done was enough to qualify me for the position, and offered me the job. I couldn't believe my luck; it would never have happened in Germany.

I ended up with a healthy annual grant and a youth centre to run. I had my own office and workshops fully equipped for pottery, screen-printing and photography. I threw myself wholeheartedly into making a success of it. I knew what it was like to be a social outcast and how it felt to be on the wrong side of the law, so I knew what would appeal to my clientele. Within weeks, I had dozens of unemployed youth signed up and creativity was flourishing. They made bongs in the pottery workshop and printed their opinion about the world on T-shirts in the print-making studio. I also organised legal workshops for them which used role-playing to educate them about their rights if they were harassed by the police or busted for drugs.

Twelve months into the job, I thought I was fulfilling the objectives perfectly. The participants were off the street, developing their creative skills, being educated in their legal rights and gaining self-esteem. However, when they began to apply their new-found legal skills, the police were not impressed and the trouble started. My name would constantly crop up as the main instigator behind their 'skilled and trained' responses and it wasn't long before I attracted unwelcome attention. In the opinion of the police, I was encouraging the local youth to be lawless and subversive and I was a troublemaker.

I looked like a drug user so they figured I must have drugs stashed at home. If they could bust me, I would be out of sight and out of mind and the problem would be solved. The first time they raided my place, they kicked the door in at 3:00 a.m., stormed into the bedroom, shone flashlights in my face and screamed at me. They turned the house upside down. Then they sat me in a chair in the kitchen and told me that I was going to prison. They gave graphic descriptions of what would happen to a pretty blue-eyed blond boy like me in jail. It was a humiliating experience. They were playing a power game and I didn't understand the rules. I would regularly turn up at their favourite pub drunk and stoned and would make a point of annoying them. I learned the hard way that this was not how you interacted with police in Australia. They raided my place two more times but never found anything. The feud escalated until my solicitor heard on the grapevine that they were intending to plant heroin on me. He advised me to leave town immediately. In an instant my world collapsed. It was like Germany all over again and I felt that I had failed again, but the prospect of going to jail terrified me and I got the first train out.

Opting out

I headed north to join my family, who'd moved to coastal Queensland, and, not knowing what else to do, I found work as a tomato picker. Each morning I would go off to the fields with a group of international backpackers. We would get paid for what we picked and as soon as we had earned enough to drink for the rest of the day we would slow down. After work we would all go to the pub and get very, very drunk and then go to the beach and get very, very stoned.

I just wanted to feel good, and a mixture of the local rum and marijuana did the trick nicely. I rented a house on the beach with a group of friends and we spent days floating on our surfboards in the warm, flat ocean. We would tow an ice-packed esky out with us so we could drink cold beer without having to go back to the house. My life became one big party. I don't remember a single Saturday or Sunday morning when I woke up in my own bed. It would always be on the floor in someone's lounge, in bed with someone, or next to my bicycle on the grass outside the pub.

I lived carelessly and spontaneously until I began to get terrible hangovers that made work in the hot sun the next morning unbearable. Then one day, as I was bending over a row of tomatoes, I was overcome with waves of dizziness and nausea so strong that I collapsed. One of my co-workers had to take me to the doctor. Even though it was a big drinking town, the doctor was shocked by the amount of alcohol and drugs I consumed. He said that fifteen beers and several joints a day was way too much and that if he drank even half of what I did, he would probably be dead. He gave me vitamin B6 and a prescription for tranquillisers and sent me home.

Counselling work

This incident was a wake-up call for me. I stopped the drinking and drugs and I found a job as a youth worker for the local Department of Family Services. This time I decided that I was going to be professional and distanced. I dedicated myself to trying to help the kids but it proved to be a hopeless task. Poverty, abuse and violence were endemic in the town. I often had to go and get children from pubs where their mothers had left them, or deal with teenagers who had been savagely abused and were themselves violent.

Once I had to go with a social worker to collect a baby boy whose mother had disappeared three days earlier, leaving him in a house with three violent, heavily tattooed and muscled men who had just got out of jail. They had no idea what to do with a baby and by the time we arrived the child had been screaming for hours. One of the men had been trying to give it hash to keep it quiet, and another threw a cushion at the child while we were there. He was deliberately trying to provoke us into starting a fight and it was tough to remain calm and friendly.

I had seen some pretty bad things in the drug squats in Amsterdam and even in my previous experience as a project officer, but what I came across in this small coastal town affected me much more deeply. It was a desperate, depressing and often frightening environment to work in. After around twelve months I took up drinking again to try to counter the hopelessness of the work and also to suppress the realisation that when I wasn't working I felt dead inside. As long as I drank I could appear to be happy and social. Alcohol and then marijuana became my support structure again.

After a couple of years I was going through a six-pack of beer and several glasses of wine each week night and up to twenty beers on Saturday and Sunday nights with tequila chasers. I would drink sociably with groups of people, or alone so I could sink into my pain. My family, who still saw me as a hopeless drug addict and loser, now decided that I was also an alcoholic. They would constantly try to make me admit I had a problem with alcohol. I knew I didn't but I was too unsure about myself to take them on. Their ongoing criticism just made me drink more and my subsequent behaviour ended up confirming everything they thought about me.

A FAMILY DINNER PARTY

I stopped at the pub on the way home from work. It was my mother's birthday and I was supposed to be going to a family dinner for her. I was not looking forward to it as I knew sooner or later someone would begin criticising me, because they always did. I had half a dozen nice cold beers to fortify myself, hoping it would allow me to appear social and at ease. Then I decided I was too inebriated and needed to snap out of it so, applying some bizarre form of logic, I went out the back with one of my drinking buddies and had a joint. Just my luck, it was Purple Heads (a *very* potent strain of marijuana) and I became instantly highly stoned. In my paranoid state it seemed logical to try to counter this with shots of tequila, so I went back to the bar.

By the time I turned up at the dinner I was late, stoned off my face and reeking of alcohol. My family were all nicely dressed and sitting around the table having a special fondue meal. A relative who was visiting from Germany had bought an expensive bottle of wine to mark the occasion and with a disapproving look he poured me a small glass. I tossed it back enthusiastically and poured myself another much larger glass, which I also drank quickly.

Feeling quite cheery I decided it was time for some food. After many failed attempts, in which morsels of food went skidding off the plate onto the white tablecloth, I managed to spear something with my fondue fork. I carefully dipped it into in the pot in the centre of the table and then leant back to aid the precarious return trip to my mouth. The weight of the fork was all it took to throw me off balance and I fell back in my chair to the floor where I promptly passed out with fondue all over my chin.

DEPRESSION

There were many more instances like this, too many, and eventually the draining nature of the work combined with years of drugs, booze and then a devastating personal tragedy was all too much. I ended up physically, emotionally and spiritually wrecked. I knew I had to change something. I gave up the dope, again, and cut back drastically on the alcohol but instead of feeling better the old emptiness that I had originally banished with marijuana and all those other drugs came back into my life. This time it was much more intense.

An unholy alliance of paranoia, fear, anxiety, guilt and hopelessness arose in me and I had periods of depression so intense that for a long time my first thought on waking was death. I would make myself get up and move but I constantly thought about suicide. Each day I would wonder whether I would make it through, or whether it would be the day I would die. It got so bad at times that I couldn't walk across bridges because I felt compelled to run to the edge and throw myself over. If I was driving and saw a truck coming towards me, a powerful urge to drive straight into it at full speed would overwhelm me and I would have to grip the steering wheel with all my strength and desperately focus on staying on my side of the road until it passed.

For the first time, I clearly understood the full implications of what I had done to myself by taking drugs. The worst part was thinking that I was going to be trapped in that terrible state forever. I couldn't drink myself into oblivion any more and I couldn't take drugs to suppress my pain so there was nothing I could do to make the emptiness and pain go. The shock of this realisation was so profound that it felt like a massive steel vice snapped shut around my heart. Every last shred of hope evaporated until even death no longer seemed a solution. I felt as if the pain was so deep it would even follow me to the grave.

To avoid alcohol and drugs I stopped socialising, and at work I just went through the motions. There was no joy in my life and I lost my belief that what I was doing was even worthwhile. It had become blatantly obvious that nothing I did was going to make the slightest bit of difference. The sheer scale of the social dysfunction was overwhelming. It was a hopeless and thankless task. I felt defeated and purposeless. I was empty and working in a job where I was surrounded by emptiness.

By now it was the late eighties, the start of the antidepressant era and several of my colleagues, who were psychologists or social workers, suggested I try antidepressants but I knew that this wouldn't really help. It would only mask the underlying problem. Besides, I'd done my drugs and if I was going to take antidepressants I might as well just do speed again and be done with it, because in the long run for me, I knew the outcome wasn't going to be much different.

I was a drug expert by then. I had over ten years of empirical evidence to draw upon and I knew that the better a drug made you feel, the worse you were going to feel afterwards and whether the drug was legal or illegal made no difference whatsoever. We had abused plenty of prescription drugs in the past, from Valium to heavy-duty painkillers, and in the end you always felt worse than you did before you took them. It was my quest to get higher and higher on drugs that had brought me to this point and from here I knew I was going to have to find my way back through my own devices rather than taking more drugs.

Somewhere underneath my pain I still had a glimmer of hope that things would improve. It was enough to make me keep moving. My first breakthrough came one day when I swam twenty laps of a pool and, to my utter astonishment, got out feeling really, really good, the kind of good that I thought only drugs could generate. The discovery that I could get there myself by doing something healthy was an awakening for me. It was my first ever insight into the fact that there was something within me that could make me feel good. This was the day my true inner journey began. I developed a new passion for fitness and health and I left my job and moved to Brisbane to study Traditional Chinese Medicine. It was the best thing I could have done.

THE STIMULANT CENTURY

Many years later, after I graduated and became a therapist, I started seeing more and more patients who had been prescribed antidepressants for 'conditions' including severe anxiety and depression. They had come to me seeking alternative remedies as many had felt even more depressed, if not suicidal, after taking medication. It made me think again about my instinctive rejection of the idea of taking antidepressants when I was depressed. I knew then that anti-depressants couldn't solve my problems; no drug could do that. If drugs were able to solve psychological problems I would have been the happiest, healthiest person on the planet because I had taken the best drugs out there for a long time.

All the hard drugs I took, even LSD, were developed or dis-covered for their therapeutic value, not for fun. LSD was the psychological 'wonder drug' of the 1960s. It was believed that it could radically change the individual—and by extension the world—by 'deconditioning' patients from limiting beliefs and neuroses (Pinchbeck 2002, pp. 179–180). A century earlier cocaine was being hailed as a wonder drug with a 'miraculous tonic effect'. It was used to treat conditions includ-ing sea-sickness, head colds and opium addiction. It was freely available and you could buy it over the counter. However, once it was discovered how addictive and destructive the drug really was, it fell from favour (Streatfeild 2001, p. 85).

Then the amphetamines, a group of synthetic stimulants introduced in the 1920s, appeared to be the new miracle drugs. They too were widely prescribed and dispensed. By 1967, in the USA alone, prescriptions for amphetamine reached a peak of 31 million (Anglin et al. 2000). Speed too was considered perfectly safe, until it was discovered that it wasn't curing anything but just making people feel good tem-porarily. Afterwards side effects from paranoid delusions to serious depression arose (Streatfeild 2001, p. 209). Like cocaine, speed became a street drug. Around that time the SSRI antidepressants, powerful new mood- and mind-altering drugs, many of which also had 'dangerously stimulating effects' (Breggin 2001, p. 30), had emerged.

ANTIDEPRESSANTS

Antidepressants are psychotherapeutic drugs that are used to relieve the symptoms of depression. They were first developed in the 1950s and have been used regularly since then. The selective serotonin reuptake inhibitors (SSRIs) such as Prozac, Zoloft and Paxil, a new class of antidepressants, are currently amongst the best selling drugs in the world. In 2000, more than 35 million people had taken Prozac (Breggin 2001, p. 1). Use of antidepressants of all types is escalating. In 2002 in Australia, within a population of 20 million people, nearly 20 million prescriptions were written for various antidepressants (AIHW 2003).

New research is now confirming that in many cases use of some antidepressants is linked to a worsened state of health. A recent investigation, using both published and unpublished data, of the risk–benefit profile of SSRIs in childhood depression has suggested that overall, the risks of many SSRIs outweigh the benefits (Whittington et al. 2004). In March 2004 the USA Food and Drug Administration asked manufacturers of many antidepressant drugs, including Prozac and Zoloft, to include in their labeling a warning statement that recommends close observation of adult and paediatric patients treated with these agents for worsening depression or the emergence of suicidality (FDA 2004).

Many of my patients who had been taking SSRI antidepressants felt just like I did after using speed. In fact their pulses indicated similar imbalances to those generated by illicit stimulant drugs. Given that SSRIs 'most closely resemble stimulant drugs such as methamphetamine, ecstasy or cocaine in most of their clinical effects' (Breggin 2001, p. 49) the similarity made sense. The underlying problem or imbalance that had caused the patient's initial anxiety or depression had not been addressed; the symptoms had just been suppressed by medication.

Nonetheless, if a patient presents to me whilst currently on medication such as antidepressants, I never interfere with that in any way. This issue frequently arises in complementary medicine. People often make an appointment when they have already reached a crisis point and have been prescribed medication. These patients then ask whether they should continue the pharmaceutical drugs or seek alternatives. In these circumstances I never suggest rejecting or discontinuing any form of medication that has been prescibed by a medical professional. Prescription drugs can move a patient out of an acute phase allowing them the 'time' and 'space' to then look at their health in a fully rounded manner.

CAUSES OF DEPRESSION

Due to my training in Traditional Chinese Medicine I believe that any 'conditions', including depression, arise from an underlying imbalance of some sort in the organs and Energy Field. Identifying rather than suppressing this is crucial for full recovery and repair. Just as my drug experiences had proved useful in my work as a therapist so too did my intimate knowledge of depression. In my own life and in scores of cases, I have observed depression arising because of the

need to 'retreat' to preserve the Yin and avoid serious pat
ogy; depression arising primarily as a result of deficiencies,
such as Spleen, Kidney, Blood or Chi deficiency; and combinations of these causes.

Faster and faster: Yin depletion depression

Humans are destined to progress. In the West however, we
have become a society that meets this primal need by chasing external goals that are often work-related. We want faster
computers, more information, quicker responses. These
desires all result from the Yang 'advance and act' stimulus, but
we have simultaneously lost the Yin ability to 'retreat and
wait'. We can't even wait in traffic or in queues anymore
without becoming frustrated and we are naturally attracted
to the stimulant drugs such as cocaine, speed and caffeine—
all of which make us go faster, but further deplete the Yin.

This desire to 'advance and act' is natural but if it is not
balanced by 'retreat and wait', by supporting material goals
with regular practice of an inner energy technique for example, the Yang will consume the Yin. Our 21st century over-
stimulated lifestyle is now consuming the Yin to a level
where it is becoming pathological. Over the past decade I
have seen increasing numbers of patients, primarily successful business people, for whom this imbalance is so far
advanced that they are unable to relax, sleep or eat, resulting
in the development of depression.

The continuation of life itself is dependant on Yin and Yang
being balanced as a complete separation of the two would
mean death. The body has mechanisms to prevent this total
separation occurring. Depression can forcibly initiate 'retreat
and wait' in order to avoid action that can no longer be

supported. I have been so depressed that I have been barely able to move, or even get out of bed. This forced me to stop going any further down the path of destruction and to pay attention to my health; I had no choice. However, if you do not pay attention to the signs, it can result in even more serious pathologies, seizures, nervous breakdowns or heart attacks.

Organ depletion depression

Poor diet can also eventually lead to depression by depleting the organs and Jing. I would argue that hundreds of millions of people who do not use illegal drugs nevertheless create imbalances through inappropriate eating habits. For example, many business people are 'too busy' to have breakfast and then have sweet biscuits for morning tea; they are too busy for a proper lunch so they grab some hot chips or a sandwich and eat it at their desk. Then they eat a large dinner late at night to try to make up for it.

Eating inappropriately is an organ-depleting behaviour that leads to major imbalances just as drug use does. Post-natal depression arises in many cases because the mother either dieted excessively for years prior to the pregnancy, becoming Blood deficient in the process, or dieted after giving birth to 'lose weight'. This is an extremely unhealthy practice for both mother and child. In women, the Jing is stored in the uterus and is used to nurture the child through pregnancy. At the moment of childbirth, part of the mother's Jing is given to the child. The stronger this is, the more the baby benefits. Some Jing is also considered to be lost in the placenta, which is why in many traditional cultures part of the placenta is consumed. Production of breast milk also draws on the Jing of the mother, leading to further loss.

I have seen many women in my clinic who, after having a child, found themselves feeling sick, exhausted or depressed due to Jing depletion. Ideally, to prevent this increasingly common occurrence, women should be on an intensive Chi, Jing and blood-building program before and after childbirth and should also be able to spend as long as necessary recovering from the birth. However, in our time-starved culture, where most of us are living beyond our energetic means, this rarely happens.

Our organs create our reality and they are dependant on nutrient intake to function properly. So, the more ambitious you are, the more you need to apply intelligence to the food you eat, in terms of quality, quantity and timing. Whether you want to be a corporate success or a happy parent of a thriving child you need to boost your organs with nutrient saturation, otherwise you will end up drawing from your Jing to meet your goals. This will accelerate the ageing process and you will quickly gravitate towards ill health and depression.

☯ CASE STUDY: DEPRESSION

The majority of patients I treat for depression, and many other organ imbalances, have no concept of the crucial role their organs play in their ability to achieve their dreams or how important the integration of body and mind is. I had a patient, Pam, presenting with depression that was, in her mind, initially due to the actions of a weak and manipulative new boss. But upon further investigation I discovered that, long before this event, like many successful people, Pam had fallen into the habit of ignoring the body in favour of the mind. It was this that had prepared the ground for what was to follow.

Pam was 26, intelligent and successful. She was a producer working in the television industry. She said that her life was great until the new boss started. The woman was less qualified than most of her staff and in Pam's view, she destroyed what had been a successful team of creative people. Important projects that Pam had underway were cancelled, funding that Pam had fought for was withdrawn and allocated to other, less interested staff members. The commitments that Pam had made were ignored and she felt her professional reputation had been compromised. She was then assigned tasks which were doomed to fail but when she tried to explain why failure was inevitable, her professional opinion was ignored.

To make matters worse, the new boss would routinely sabotage what Pam was doing, either deliberately or through ignorance. Pam became highly anxious and stressed. She couldn't eat and developed insomnia and irritability. When she got to the stage where she felt physically ill just at the thought of going to work, she went to seek medical help. The doctor diagnosed her as being depressed due to a chemical imbalance in the brain and prescribed an SSRI antidepressant in conjunction with cognitive behavioural therapy.

At first the medication made her feel worse but after around a month Pam noticed that she was feeling quite happy. The antidepressants seemed to take the edge off everything. Work situations that a few weeks ago would have seemed like huge problems now seemed quite minor. She felt like she was running on a higher level of energy and was more sociable, chatty and communicative than she would have normally been. She felt more 'gung-ho' than normal and was prepared to take risks again due to her impression that because she wasn't really 'herself', nothing really mattered.

Twelve months later Pam believed that her life was back on track and under control again. She phoned her doctor who suggested that Pam phase out the antidepressants. After a couple of weeks of feeling very ill, Pam then felt permanently 'flat'. Then the old symptoms came creeping back: the insomnia, anxiety, panic attacks, lack of appetite . . . now she was also getting trapped in extreme behaviour patterns. Her irritation developed into fury at the smallest setbacks. In her sex life she alternated between excess and abstinence. The feeling that she couldn't get sexual satisfaction, even if she had orgasm after orgasm, would alternate with feeling outraged when her husband dared to touch her. She was exhausted, constantly felt like crying and had a debilitating sense of worthlessness.

Work seemed like a nightmare again. She was convinced that everything she did was going to fail so there was no point doing anything. She didn't want to talk to anyone because she was sure that everything she said would sound stupid. She felt worse each day until it reached the point where she couldn't get out of bed because she felt she was going to make a mess of absolutely everything. She would lie there physically unable to even move while her mind raced with negative thoughts. When she started thinking of suicide she came to see me.

Pam felt that the 'chemical imbalance in her brain' must have recurred and was hoping I could offer a means of redressing this by natural means as she didn't want to take antidepressants again. I explained that in Traditional Chinese Medicine we don't look at symptoms in isolation, but rather work with the whole person and that I would start by using pulse diagnosis to get a picture of her general health, constitutional type and inner energy. Pulse diagnosis, when executed properly, can reveal the state of your organs and thus your true state of health.

Diagnosis

I identified Pam as having a Yang constitution and a strong need to achieve. These types need to be active in pursuing their goals and dreams because if they are blocked from achieving their potential, they can easily become frustrated. Accordingly, a pre-requisite for Pam to be healthy and happy was an environment in which her skills and talents could be used. As might be expected, there were signs in her pulse that Liver Chi was not flowing freely, indicating that she was frustrated by an inability to advance and 'expand' in accord with her nature. She was also presenting symptoms of serious organ deficiency and Blood and Chi deficiencies which would be linked to her depression.

We discussed her previous work history in detail and she said that she committed herself 100 percent to projects and would do whatever it took to ensure that they were done perfectly. She prided herself on never making mistakes. She often worked weekends and holidays without pay and did not stop to eat or relax. She couldn't understand what she termed 'the bludgers' in her workplace: people who constantly had coffee breaks, took long lunches and exploited the system by taking sick days as they accrued whether they were sick or not. Pam worked obsessively regardless of how she felt and never took sick days or holidays. The industry was fast-paced and she didn't want to 'miss anything' or let things get out of control.

Seeing people around her with their feet on their desks reading the paper drove her mad. 'Achievers' often react to 'bludgers' in this way because achievers need to work hard. This is usually a result of their Yang constitution, their social conditioning or both, and while it can make them hard-working employees or successful entrepreneurs, it can also lead to serious depletion. In one sense, the workers who Pam referred to as 'bludgers' have better developed Yin, due to their lifestyle. They don't over-tax their systems, because they take regular breaks, meals and days off. Accordingly they are able to enjoy passive states of sitting back and doing nothing. Pam couldn't do this even if she wanted to.

The depleted state of her organs indicated that she would have experienced some of the pathological symptoms arising from this lifestyle well before the new boss arrived. When I asked how she felt on weekends or on her days off before the new boss started, Pam said that she never really enjoyed time off but couldn't understand why and didn't really have time to think about it.

I explained that this was a warning sign that organ deple-tion was already underway and that the Yin was being consumed. The symptoms of this underlying depletion had not manifested fully prior to the change in workplace man-agement because in the past, under her old boss, she had been able to use her skills, achieve her goals and her successes were acknowledged. Accordingly Chi was moving relatively freely during work hours and she felt satisfied and happy. Her will-power, desire to succeed and the positive feedback had been suppressing her symptoms, but it was only a matter of time before her imbalances would catch up with her. By inhibiting her ability to progress or 'expand' at work the new boss was simply a catalyst for this inevitable health crisis.

Jing, Yin and Kidney Chi

In a situation where what I term an 'external inhibitor', such as Pam's new boss, blocks a person's ability to expand, it is best to 'retreat and wait', or to step back, consider your options and then act accordingly. To be able to do this though you need strong Kidney Chi, Yin and Jing. These give you 'backbone', will-power and self-esteem so you don't feel threatened by the actions of the inhibitor. Of all these, Jing is the principal reserve with which to bounce back after defeat (Hammer 1991, p. 302).

Pam had spent years studying and working hard without the physical lifestyle necessary to support this mental activity. She had not supported her professional goals with Yin enhancing activities such as creating a buffer zone before she went to work, eating a proper lunch away from work, resting appropriately and using inner energy techniques to learn how to keep Liver Chi flowing in the face of obstacles. So she did not have such reserves of inner strength. The year on anti-depressants may have appeared to stabilise her moods, but afterwards she was even more depleted and her depression worsened.

SSRI ANTIDEPRESSANTS INTERPRETED USING TRADITIONAL CHINESE MEDICINE

The SSRI antidepressant she had been prescibed had a stimulant nature and, as I explained to Pam, if its action was interpreted from the perspective of Traditional Chinese Medicine, it could be said that it drew upon her Jing to regu-late the flow of the Liver Chi, so that she would accept the external situation. Thus the drug created the impression that the inhibition was not taking place and that she was continuing to progress and expand. This gave her a false sense of happiness and self-worth. When she decided to stop taking antidepressants her Liver Chi flow was no longer being artificially regulated so she felt anger and frustration. In addition, the depletion of her Jing and organs meant she now had nothing left to draw upon internally. This was why suicide was starting to look like an option.

DEPRESSION TREATMENT

I told Pam that we could change this situation by repairing her organs and building Chi, Blood and Jing. Then positive emotions could manifest again, her self-esteem would rise and she would be able to deal with her toxic work environment or any future inhibitors in a non-destructive manner. She would also be able to think clearly and creatively again and perhaps consider alternative work options. Pam seemed quite surprised by this last suggestion, but as I explained to her, if you have drive, ambition and skill but are in an environment in which these are not used and will in fact be blocked, you will never be happy, regardless of how healthy you are. An organism that cannot expand effectively is dying from within.

It takes a long time to repair the degree of damage that Pam had unknowingly inflicted upon herself and in an ideal world her recovery would take place at a holistic retreat that could address every aspect of her health—physical, spiritual and psychological—for as long as necessary. However, in reality Pam had a mortgage and needed to return to work as soon as possible. So, the first step was high-energy Bodywork which would provide her with an instant experience of free-flowing Chi or wellbeing again. Her total depletion had trapped her into immobility on every level and the Bodywork would kickstart her progress upwards preventing her from sliding further down into depression.

I also prescribed powerful nutritional supplements and emphasised the fact that every meal she ate now had to count, because once you get to the stage of depletion and depression that she had, you can't afford any actions which will further deplete you. Everything you do has to contribute to repair and food is a crucial part of this. Pam had not eaten breakfast for months, was eating sandwiches at her desk for lunch and rarely bothered with dinner. I wrote a list of options for each meal for her and asked her to make sure these meals were consumed at a leisurely pace in a peaceful environment away from work.

In addition I also suggested that she try Kung-fu because she had a fighting nature which she needed to get in touch with again, but also because martial arts teach how to 'advance' in the presence of Yin. Once you learn this you can apply it in daily life and be able to deal with inhibitors without harming yourself. If you are an achiever you will meet with inhibitors, it is the nature of things. So it is essential to learn how to respond to them.

Pam loved the idea of Kung-fu. She took up a class that same week and said later that it had really been a turning point for her. The physical exercise, where she had to concentrate on her breathing and on the movements of her body made her feel that she had taken control of her body again. She felt grounded, and had a realisation that this physical unit was her and that she had to take care of it. I explained to Pam that martial arts bring the mind back into the body. In a state of depression the mind feels separated from the body. The mind feels frantically active and the body feels slow and heavy. Martial arts redress this imbalance, but to truly reap the benefits of this body–mind training you need a lifestyle dedicated to health and wellbeing on every level.

Helping Pam understand her nature or constitution was another important component of my treatment. Pam knew that she was by nature competitive and liked success but she said that in conjunction with the antidepressants she had been undertaking cognitive behavioural therapy and the psychologist had suggested she repeat to herself 'it's alright to fail, it's alright to fail'. Pam had great difficulty accepting this at the time because 'failure' in anything went against her very nature but also, because she was on the antidepressant when she saw the psychologist, she was feeling artificially exuberant so she felt there was no need to follow this advice anyway.

I explained that Western medicine had made a connection between her relentless drive and ambition: her Yang nature, and her depression. Repeating to herself 'it's alright to fail' was a strategy to force her into a passive mental state; a Yin state. However, I saw her ambition and drive as an asset, but one that required maintenance in terms of learning to balance Yang with Yin. The program I devised for her was designed to integrate body, mind and spirit so that she could realise her potential and achieve the great things I believed she was destined for.

Black sheep, white sheep

Pam's case fascinated me. She was the total opposite to me: she had studied hard and done well at school and at university. She had never broken the law or taken an illicit drug in her life. She had achieved every goal, never stuffed up a job, she was balanced and calm and always did the right thing. She was the 'white sheep' of her family. I was the 'black sheep' of mine. Yet our different paths had led us both to exactly the same point of suicidal depression. It just didn't seem right.

But this clearly illustrates two simple but important points. The first is that any mood- or mind-altering drug, whether legal or illegal, is fundamentally the same in terms of the destruction it wreaks on the body, mind and spirit. Secondly, if you don't learn how to live you will become sick.

CHAPTER SEVEN

Starting the inner journey

ENDORPHINS AND EXERCISE

After my 'pool epiphany' I thought exercise was the answer to all my problems. But the depression lingered just beneath the surface and if I wasn't busy doing something, it would rise and consume me. So I just kept moving. Soon I was running, swimming and cycling in the morning and then weight-training with aerobic exercises in the evening. I competed in triathlons and other races. After a while I looked fit, tanned and healthy, but I found that in between working out or competing, usually mid-morning and mid-afternoon, I would get intense spells of lethargy and fatigue.

In my morning counselling sessions with the kids, I had moments when I couldn't focus on what they were saying or worse still, I'd be unable to stop yawning. My eyelids felt like lead and all I wanted to do was sleep. By lunchtime I usually felt slightly better but by mid-afternoon I would have serious problems staying awake. One afternoon I had to pick up two kids from the police station. I arrived ten minutes early so I took a seat in the reception area. It was around 3.00 pm and very hot. I had done a heavy training session that morning and within minutes the lethargy overwhelmed me. The next thing I knew, I was being woken by one of the kids shaking my arm. All that exercise was supposed to be making me fit and healthy, not so fatigued that I would sleep on the job.

ENDORPHINS

Endorphins are biochemicals, which were first discovered in the 1960s through research in a number of independent laboratories. Endorphins are thought to be produced in the brain and released as a natural response to stress, modifying or blocking the way nerve cells transmit pain signals. They have a similar 'analgesic' or pain-reducing effect to opiates and other artificial painkillers—and can result in similar patterns of tolerance and addiction with repeated exposure. A well-known example of endorphin release is the mild euphoria triggered by prolonged physical stress, which is commonly known as 'runner's high'.

The problem with my exercise program was that I was fit for competition but not for life because I was chasing the feeling of endorphin release. It had replaced drugs for me and I couldn't get enough of it. I had become trapped in another higher and higher cycle where I felt good if I exercised but had to deal with overwhelming fatigue, a version of 'coming down', a couple of hours after I finished. So I did more and more exercise. However, endorphins are only released after you force yourself to push through your pain barriers, and if you keep doing this excessively it will create imbalances.

I remember once seeing a well-known athlete win a gruelling five-hour surf race. As he triumphantly crossed the finish line, his wife ran out to congratulate him. He reacted by aggressively pushing her away. At the time I was as surprised as the rest of the spectators but later on, after I had studied Traditional Chinese Medicine, I understood that the race had exhausted all his Yin qualities and turned him temporarily into an unpredictable Yang-driven organism for whom 'advance and act' was the only option. He simply didn't have the Yin necessary to be able to stop and embrace his wife. I was starting to see evidence of this unreasonable behaviour in myself as well and I didn't like it.

THERAPEUTIC EXERCISE

I now believe that competitive exercise is not particularly beneficial to health as, in order to win, people often push harder than their constitution would naturally allow. Such persistence to keep on moving forward regardless of discomfort can over-develop Yang, in particular the Liver Yang which is necessary to generate the surges of 'advance and act' needed for winning. This consumes the Yin and if this imbalance is not addressed, it can eventually manifest either in conditions such as chronic fatigue syndrome or in emotional Yang excess states such as anger or short attention-span. For anyone bent on achieving goals, Yang qualities, in particular Liver Yang, are crucial, but for happiness and health, they need to be balanced with Yin qualities.

EXERCISE AND EMOTIONAL RELEASE MECHANICS

If you move beyond the desire for purely physical goals such as winning races or setting records, endurance exercise can have a therapeutic effect. With the correct intent and in the correct environment, it can initiate the breakdown of blockages in the Human Energy Field and release the associated stored emotions. For this to occur though you need to focus on what is happening internally rather than distracting yourself by watching TV, reading a magazine or chatting to fellow exercisers.

Body–Mind therapy is based on the idea that emotions are energy in motion. Because energy can't be destroyed, if it can't move the body stores it in the form of obstructions or distortions in the Energy Field. These blockages occur at the acupuncture points that resonate with the psycho-emotional nature of the underlying cause and they make the surrounding muscles contract around the blocked acupuncture point. Accordingly, stored or repressed emotions affect you not only mentally, but physically as well.

Certain emotions are stored in certain muscle groups. Generally speaking the chest stores issues of grief and sadness. The centre of the chest relates to Heart and love issues. Pain in the posterior neck and shoulder muscle group, which 'carry the load' of life, is often related to stress issues. The lower back stores fear, and tightness here can be connected to 'taking on too many responsibilities'. Fear issues can also manifest as weak or stiff legs, in particular weak and sore knees. Issues to do with excessive thinking, obsession and boundary setting are stored in the solar plexus and thus affect the abdominal area and often create symptoms including nausea, sluggish digestion and cravings for sweets. Unresolved anger is stored in the muscles of the middle back, hips and thighs.

ON THE TREADMILL

After ten minutes of running on the treadmill at a fast pace, my breath was ragged, my muscles were burning and my mind was screaming for me to stop. I knew that in TCM pain is considered the result of a stagnation of Chi. The breath moves Chi so, theoretically, the breath can move pain. I focused on coordinating my breath with the movement of my legs. I accepted the pain and, breath by breath, sank straight into the center of it. I tried to become one with my legs and my hips. The pain became stronger as I increased the pace and I sank into it more deeply, still focusing on 'acceptance'.

Gradually this began to work. Heat waves moved up and down my legs transforming blockages into free flow. I felt as if I was running on thick cushions. The Chi flowed through my torso, neck, shoulders and arms and I became an energy field moving in space. It was fantastic. Suddenly, an image of a close female relative screaming at me, 'You are a fucked-up, drugged-out hippie!' flashed into my mind. 'Face the truth, you are totally fucked-up like so many of your drug-crazed generation. You need to work hard because you still need a lot of development. Maybe in your next life you can move up from your low level.

It is my job to tell you the truth, why don't you admit that you are fucked-up? You live in an illusion.'

I couldn't get it out of my head and it destroyed any equilibrium I had achieved, replacing it with rage and frustration. In my mind I screamed back at her, telling her what a mess she was. How she spent all her time criticising other people but had never achieved anything herself. I became more and more angry. I felt my fists clenching and my shoulders lifting. The anger supplied me with energy, which took over the labour of the physical work. I was no longer aware that I was running. I was now fixated on retaliation.

Then some other part of my mind cut in, making me realise that the surfacing of all this intense emotion was the result of a de-obstruction in my Energy Field. Suppressed emotions were being released. Even in my infuriated state I knew that this was an opportunity to work on letting go of these tormenting and destructive memories and converting them into freeflowing energy. It was up to me to take that liberating step. How to do it though?

In desperation, I had once asked a spiritual teacher about how to deal with this problem. According to his philosophy, 'people with a sharp tongue' are the universe's way of creating an environment for 'burning karma' as they take on the karma of the people they criticise. So we should bless them and be grateful, as they can set us free. The challenge is to accept critical people as an opportunity for liberation and not to take their opinions personally. They usually don't have any real insight and their diatribes are often generated by their own imbalances or a projection of their own fears onto others. 'Accept them, send them love and keep on moving forward, in this way you let go of your karma,' were his words.

Even though this relative now lived on the other side of the world and we had a very different relationship, this destructive 'virtual' argument kept re-running in my mind and I was desperate to rid myself of it. I'd never been able to stand my ground with the person in real life, but when these scenes replayed in my head, although I could argue back as long as I liked and say everything I had always wanted to, it gave me no relief. My mind would just create even more inflammatory dialogue for her, which made me more angry. Even though this was all happening in my head, and I was creating it, I couldn't help getting trapped in the cycle. All it took was the memory of one critical and painful comment that she had made, and it would kick-off an interminable dialogue until I reached the point where I just wanted to scream.

This was all happening because I had resisted the original pain, and suppressed and stored the memories. Running on the treadmill created physical discomfort and psychological resistance. As I committed myself to overcoming this resistance by persisting with the endurance training, I developed the Liver Yang qualities of 'advance and act'. This, in conjunction with the monotonous movement, instigated the breakdown of blockages in my Energy Field, releasing the suppressed emotions connected with them.

However, the increased Liver Yang made me want to attack, to deal with the apparent source of the pain by any means including physical, but this wasn't an option and even if it had been, it would only have made the situation worse. Expressing anger does not mean that you are releasing 'suppressed' anger, you are just reacting in an untrained manner. The trained response is to acknowledge the pain and transmute it through acceptance. This creates freeflow.

If I translated the teacher's ideas about 'burning karma' into this kind of language, I would say that by triggering my anger, this relative was bringing my inner pain into my conscious mind. The concept of 'sending love' as the spiritual teacher had suggested, represented 'acceptance', a mechanism for transmuting the pain or 'lifting my karma'.

The very idea of 'sending love' while in this reactive and furious state sent resistance jolting through me. It seemed impossible. When I asked the teacher about this, his reply was that if I couldn't send real love I should send 'artificial love'. These internal dialogues made me so angry I couldn't imagine sending artificial love, even if I knew what that was. But I also knew that I had to deal with this issue, otherwise I wouldn't be able to move on and I would keep playing out these scenes in my head, and attracting similar people and situations in my life again and again.

From then on, whenever the dialogue in my mind started, instead of reacting in anger I constantly repeated the word 'love' in my head. I kept at it and one day when I was running, my anger vanished, the resistance diminished and in my mind's eye I could look at her face with love. I was stunned. For years she had represented pain and anger for me but now all I felt was a sensation which I could only describe as love.

My mind kicked in trying to analyse the process but it just couldn't explain what had happened so I told myself, 'Don't doubt it, just accept the positive, keep running, keep repeating "love"'. I felt something lift. This was actually working—the teacher was right, sending artificial love made the real thing eventually follow. For the first time it seemed there was a possibility of freeing myself from emotional heaviness and reaching a state where I could think of her without resentment, pain or anger. And all without drugs! My body felt lighter and lighter until I was able to run in peace with renewed confidence in the universal laws.

TRIGGER PEOPLE

I had always thought that it was only me who had this problem of endlessly arguing with someone in my head, but as a therapist I found it very common. I started researching its significance from the perspective of TCM. I discovered that in all the cases I saw, the person who set off the cycle was inevitably someone who had constantly denigrated or criticised the ideas or actions of my patients and blocked their ability to progress so severely that it created imbalances in their Energy Fields. I coined the term 'trigger person' (TP) to describe this person. A title in line with the Bodywork term 'trigger point', a point which triggers an involuntary reaction in the muscles, which can be used to release energetic obstructions. Interestingly, all patients immediately related to the term 'trigger person', although they were not familiar with the Bodywork concept.

Criticising and attacking others is very easy to do. In Body–Mind therapy it is considered that what we criticise in others is actually directed at ourselves, so by criticising others we satisfy the need to acknowledge our own weaknesses and temporarily alleviate our own frustrations. But this is not healthy behaviour, and unless we look within and commit ourselves to change any one of us can easily become a trigger person for other people.

Anyone who has a strong influence on your personal or professional development can become a TP, but family members are likely candidates as they influence you during your formative years. In these cases after you reach adulthood you may find yourself feeling powerless, lacking self-worth and reacting negatively to people who you perceive as being in positions of authority. Each time you do this though it adds to the blockage originally caused by the TP. Eventually it reaches crisis point, the TP moves into your head and the virtual battle begins.

It can become so intense that you feel they are living in your head. Whenever you are by yourself, doing something monotonous or repetitive like driving a car or jogging, the TP appears and generates anger, aggression and a heated internal dialogue. If you are in a relationship, your partner knows all about your TP, because you have told him or her all about them during hours of accusations, blame and analysis. But constantly talking about it doesn't help—on the contrary it fuels and intensifies the anger and negativity and feeds the cycle.

☯ CASE STUDY: TRIGGER PEOPLE

A past patient, Susan, a middle-aged school teacher, had come to see me regarding anxiety, panic attacks and breathing problems that had developed after her mother had died. It turned out that her mother's death had also created a major drama between Susan and her brother and he had become a TP for her. The reading of the will had started the problem as, although it divided their mother's estate equally between the two of them, Susan's brother took anything he thought was valuable for himself, including a ring which Susan's mother had bequeathed to her.

Susan tried to tell herself that it wasn't important, but at the same time she felt it was really unfair and she wanted to demand the ring back, but she just couldn't. This inability to act made her angry. In her professional life she would often find herself in situations where, in the presence of domineering or authoritative men, she would feel paralysed, speak hesitantly and be unable to voice dissenting opinions. She hated that aspect of herself—she was a professional adult—and couldn't understand her own behaviour.

Susan's brother was ten years older than her and had taken on the authority of a parent, rather than a sibling. He had lived at home until he was over thirty, to save money and invest in property, so despite the age difference he was at home throughout her childhood and adolescence. Their mother had adored him and did everything for him. He expected Susan to do the same. He had ordered her around and bullied her throughout her childhood, demanding that she make his bed, clean his room and do his washing. As she grew up, he constantly interfered in her life and relationships. He had oppressed her natural desire to expand and develop and caused suppression of her Yang qualities.

Even when they both got on with their separate lives, the original Yang suppression was still there, stored in her body. When Susan came to see me, she had reached the point where she was constantly arguing with her brother in her head. She would scream at him things she could never say to his face: how she was the one who cared for their mother all through her illness while he was 'too busy'. She would go bushwalking to try to reduce her stress, but would find herself stomping along looking at the ground and starting the arguments again. He wasn't even there! It was driving her crazy.

Susan's brother was a clear example of a trigger person. His overbearing behaviour over the years had conditioned her to feel paralysed when he was around. They had established a behavioural pattern in their relationship that in TCM terms I would describe as governed by an imbalance of the Liver functions of 'advance and act' and 'retreat and wait'. When Susan saw her brother she would involuntarily fall into the passive Liver Yin excess state. But because living organisms naturally seek balance, when he was not there, in her head she would take the role of the Liver Yang excess 'aggressor' by yelling at him, and he would have the role of the Liver Yin excess 'receiver'.

But reversing the roles by displaying imaginary or even real aggression towards a TP does not correct anything or deal with the underlying relationship imbalances. The TP is in fact flagging this imbalance for you. TPs force you to identify areas in your life that require emotional, spiritual and physical growth. When the pain, anger and frustration reach the conscious mind, you have an opportunity to process them. To do this though you need to develop your Liver Yang in the context of this relationship.

Running, or other forms of endurance exercise, establish an environment in which you can do so. As soon as the TP comes into your mind, if you face and accept him or her: face and accept the associated anger and pain and repeat the word 'love', you will gradually develop the Liver Yang that you need in that relationship but not in an aggressive or angry manner. You will then find yourself changing. Eventually you will become non-reactive in the presence of your TP and this is truly liberating.

So, rather than being your worst enemy, your TP can enable you to develop inner peace. As at an even deeper level there may also be karmic issues involved, you can use the opportunity to help break a bad karmic cycle that may have been in place for generations. Accordingly, endurance exercise, which offers an opportunity to release and resolve TP issues, can be a crucial part of developing your wellbeing.

TAI-CHI AND CHI-GUNG

When I discovered Tai-chi, another crucial piece of the wellbeing puzzle fell into place. I had met a woman who was convinced that Tai-chi had changed her life and dramatically improved her health and I was inspired to try it. I knew nothing about it at the time and I imagined uniforms, drill routines and military-style instructors. But from the moment I walked in the door for my first lesson, I knew my life was going to change.

A huge banner printed with a Yin and Yang symbol hung on the far wall of the hall where the class was being held, and bamboo flute music drifted through the air. In the centre of the room a dozen or so casually dressed people were performing synchronised, fluid movements. I could feel waves of warm energy washing over me. My heart opened up and I felt that intoxicating combination of excitement and mystery that in my mind had always been associated with drugs. Feeling it in this environment was revelatory, maybe it was this that I had been seeking all along.

I stood there momentarily transfixed. Then one of the participants left the group, came over and introduced himself to me. It turned out that he was the instructor. He had long hair, bare feet and was wearing baggy pants and an old T-shirt. His bright blue eyes revealed compassion, humour and zest in equal parts and, despite his non-muscular appearance, he had an aura of true strength. I longed for some of his enthusiasm and passion. As he shook my hand I told him how graceful the moves looked and how they had evoked a sense of peace in me.

He eyed my heavily-muscled body speculatively for a moment and then said that there was more to Tai-chi than calm and peaceful-looking moves. He stepped back and started moving slowly in gentle, dance-like poses then, in a split second, his arms and legs flew with deadly, acrobatic punches and kicks accompanied by explosive yells. A second later, he resumed the slow and tranquil movements, showing no sign of breathlessness from the physical exertion. I was stunned. In just a few moments I had witnessed the transition from peacefulness to aggression, executed with perfect control. I felt another rush of excitement and I knew that if I followed what I sensed in this moment, my own life would improve.

He then gave me a brief introduction to Chi-gung, an ancient practice designed to cultivate Chi. I could feel the power of it instantly. He told me that Chi-gung translated as 'energy-work' and that it was actually more effective than medication for many illnesses. In some cases in China, people had been cured of conditions such as bone cancer purely with the practice of Chi-gung. I found an article about this when I was studying which said something like: the only side effect of treating disease with Chi-gung is personality growth and spiritual enlightenment.

CHI-GUNG

I imagined that I was suspended from a hook at the top of my head, and I bent my knees and held my arms out in front of me as if I was hugging a tree—a position familar from my hippie days! I soon felt intense discomfort in my arms and shoulders. I focused on breathing into the pain and trying to relax my shoulders but after a few minutes I felt like screaming. I now had the sensation of burning heat in my shoulders. It felt like needles were stabbing into the surrounding muscles.

Every time I exhaled I tried to sink into the increasing pain and every time I inhaled I expanded my whole being—body, mind and spirit—while merging with the pain and repeating my mantra of 'accept, accept'. The idea was to use my inner energy rather than contracted muscles to hold my arms up. But after years of weight-lifting and body-building, it was difficult to get my head around the concept of working with relaxed muscles.

By now the muscles in my arms were totally contracted and felt as heavy as lead so the stance hurt like hell. Sweat ran down my face, heat rushed through my body and my breathing was laboured. I could feel the energy pounding at my acupuncture points, attacking in particular the point near the apex of my shoulder. Every time the Chi tried to get through the pain intensified. I tried to accept the pain as I inhaled, and sink into it more deeply when I exhaled. My aim was to convert the pain into Chi flow.

Suddenly my vision altered, the foreground and background began to oscillate, forming a vibrating pattern of black and white. Although my arms were still suspended in mid-air, the muscle tremor was replaced by a deep stillness and it felt as if they were now resting on an invisible cushion. The heaviness in my legs also disappeared. Warm currents of energy moved in a circular motion through my abdominal area and along my arms and legs, enveloping my whole body in warmth. I could hear what sounded like distant fun-fair music that could have been drifting in from far away or emerging from inner dimensions.

My body felt as if it was floating, but simultaneously I felt really grounded. Objects around me lost their form and became an interplay of colours, shapes and patterns. I felt like I was tripping, but at the same time I had mental clarity and control. My breathing was effortless and deep, reaching every part of my body and delivering Chi to all organs. I had no reference to past, future or present but at the same time I knew exactly where I was. Everything made sense to me. Pain no longer existed, I was in a state of perfect freeflow.

TAI-CHI AND CHI-GUNG: THERAPEUTIC VALUE

After doing Chi-gung I always felt a similar exhilaration and euphoria to that generated by a long-distance run, but it was much more fulfilling. Instead of burning excess Yang, which creates a false sensation of relaxation after heavy exercise, I had built Yang in the presence of Yin, so I felt simultaneously relaxed and energetically fuelled and active.

The Chi-gung postures are designed to place the body in a physical configuration that puts specific acupuncture points under pressure. For example, in the Chi-gung posture of 'hugging the tree', the angle of the major joints, in combination with gravity, acts as a vice and applies pressure to the places where energy blockages are located. This pressure can break down these blockages and convert them back into moving energy. However, techniques like Chi-gung also set up an 'intelligence' that prevents the Human Energy Field from developing blockages when exposed to either external or internal inhibitors.

Tai-chi is essentially a series of Chi-gung stances that flow into one another. These are executed at a slow pace, as movement is supposed to be initiated by internal energy rather than by muscles or force. Tai-chi and Chi-gung also illustrate the interaction of the fundamental polar forces of Yin and Yang. Daily practice enabled me to explore the relationship between inhibitors, resistance, my inner pain and the flow of Chi.

Better still, with the ongoing repetition of Tai-chi and Chi-gung I began to be able to recapture at will that emotional state which in the past I could only have achieved by smoking bongs, or drinking beer. Needless to say I loved it. I had a found a new way to feel good. I added daily Tai-chi and Chi-gung to my exercise routine. I altered postures to increase the stress on the acupuncture points and maximise the therapeutic outcomes. I was riding a new wave of highs but I still had the underlying feeling that some important part of my life was missing. Then, towards the end of my first semester of college, a fellow student invited me to go to a meditation seminar with him and the final puzzle piece fell into place.

REDISCOVERING BLISS

The meditation teacher, an elderly Sikh, dressed in robes and a turban, stressed that the form of meditation he was going to conduct was based on surrender and that we would need to 'let go' in order to let the divine source within us do its work. There were about twenty people in the room and we all stood around looking vague while he intoned the mantra. As instructed I closed my eyes and let my thoughts pass just as if they were cars passing by. I tried to relax. I was not expecting much to happen but it seemed a pleasant enough way to spend a Saturday.

After a few minutes I noticed a familiar feeling of warmth in my abdominal area. It intensified until I felt an overwhelming urge to move. First I was stunned by this, but then I surrendered to the feeling, My body swayed to rhythms which I couldn't hear but knew existed. Suddenly and unexpectedly, I burst out laughing. I could sense that others in the room were having similar experiences. A sensation of bliss rushed through my body, wiping away every thought. I became completely immersed in the experience, with no need to analyse or understand it.

I started to softly clap my hands and tap my feet. Others in the room were responding similarly, and in no time most members of the group were engaged in a liberating and vigorous session of clapping, stomping and dancing. Bursts of pure energy shot through me. I was laughing and shouting and it felt great. I moved through the room. I was conscious of being an individual but I also felt that I was connected to everyone. I'd never met these people before but we were now as close as if we had all been partying together for days and had broken through all social barriers. It was the most intense celebration I had ever experienced without drugs or alcohol.

MEDITATION

There had always been some part of me that still longed for the spontaneity and effortlessness of the euphoria of my youth: of the time before the heavy drugs had ruined our spirits, when Stefan, Karl, Dietrich and I were young, healthy and innocent; when we thought we would live forever in the magical hippie world of love and brotherhood. But I had taken my last hard drug years before discovering meditation and, like most drug users, I had always believed that the instant euphoria and bonding came from the drugs and went with the drugs. The meditation session showed me that I could access joy, bonding and bliss instantaneously without drugs. This realisation was crucially important for me and I added meditation to my daily routine.

MY LAST JOINT

My past drug use had made me feel so bad that I had become obsessed with feeling good. It was this that led me to keep exercising, to taking up Chi-gung and Tai-chi, and then meditation. I had stumbled onto the path of self-realisation without even noticing. In addition, when I started studying Traditional Chinese Medicine I knew with an absolute certainty that I had found my purpose in life. Subconsciously I recognised that I was now doing something fundamentally right. I had moved forward and changed my life. Once you are on the path of self-development and constant improvement, I think your life comes into line with a bigger cosmic plan and your body starts to reject the things that will sabotage this progress.

By the time I discovered meditation I had already been exercising and doing Tai-chi and Chi-gung daily for quite a while. I hadn't touched cocaine or speed for years, and knew I never would again, but I was still occasionally smoking dope. I hadn't gone to that seminar yet that was to change the way I viewed drugs, so marijuana still seemed 'harmless' to me. I never imagined I would give it up. But drugs have a limited cycle of use: they can only deliver their highs for a certain amount of time, and sooner or later all drug users will reach the point where they either give up voluntarily or are forced to because of increasingly unpleasant side effects. This might be after one acid trip, a year of ecstasy, months of snorting cocaine or, in my case, a good decade of taking just about everything I could get my hands on.

The end of my drug journey was a bit of an anticlimax after the roller-coaster ride that they had taken me on. On the night it happened, which was just after the meditation seminar, I had been studying really hard for a major biochemistry exam and I had finally managed to memorise all the information required. I decided to 'celebrate' with a nice big joint. I was sharing a house with three other students at the time so we sat in the lounge and passed the joint around. After they went to bed I put on one of my favourite Pink Floyd albums and sat back ready to enjoy my 'reward', like I used to in the old days. But nothing happened. I was stoned but I felt totally detached from the music and from the experience of being stoned. The magic was completely gone. It was an empty experience: not good, not bad, just empty.

To add insult to injury, by the time I finally fell asleep it was 5:00 am and when I woke up it was too late to exercise, meditate or do Tai-chi before college and I felt really 'off' all day. Worse still, I couldn't recall all the facts that I had memorised for the exam. The whole week ended up being a write-off. I felt that I had lost ground, wasted valuable time, and I knew that my long and complicated relationship with drugs was finally finished.

CHAPTER EIGHT

Hitting the wall

RECAPTURING MY DREAMS

By the time I graduated from my four years of study in Traditional Chinese Medicine, I was feeling fit, energetic and healthy again. I had kept up my routine of endurance training, Tai-chi and meditation, and had also been applying all my new-found knowledge about health and therapy to myself along the way. Drugs and excessive alcohol were a thing of the past and I was on a path of constant improvement. It was time to change the world, again, so I signed a lease for a health care centre.

The New Age

Taking on a lease put me in a position where I had to make my career as a therapist a success. Knowing that I would need some form of guidance to make this new enterprise work though, and with no idea where else to turn, I saturated myself with the literature of the New Age. My introduction to this movement had occurred the early 1980s when I was inter-acting professionally with progressive community workers. We all read *The Aquarian Conspiracy*, a book celebrating new ways of thinking about vocation, spirituality and society in general, and we tried to implement this vision in our work.

In this spirit I decided that there should be nothing 'clini-cal' about my clinic and I set about refurbishing. By the time it was finished the main entrance looked like an Egyptian temple doorway, and large painted panels depicting scenes from the Egyptian Book of the Dead were featured on both the inside and outside walls of the building. The four treat-ment rooms were painted in shades of gold, pink and soft blue. The idea was to use the decor to present an atmosphere of creativity and individuality and to help send the message that health is an art which needs to be addressed creatively.

In the early days my co-workers were mainly female, mid-dle-aged psychics, art therapists and 'channelers'. They repre-sented the first wave of alternative health practitioners whose work was based on intuition, visions or channelled information. One of the more memorable dressed in saris and ate chocolates and read romance novels in between seeing patients. She eventually ran away with a man half her age and reputedly started a sex cult in India.

It was an amazing, colourful and exciting time for me. I studied Body Electronics, Body Harmony and Body Energetics, networked with other therapists, went to healing seminars and did scores of esoteric workshops including re-birthing, Reiki and past-life regression. I learned a lot about myself and satisfied my desire for a visionary element in my life, but after a while I realised that I couldn't really apply all these New Age insights and revelations to the practical concerns of managing a business. Workshops offering happiness in just three hours or claiming twelve-strand DNA to be the key to evolving into higher consciousness lost their appeal for me.

This was around the time that a distinction was forming between the hobbyists and the new wave of college graduates, many of whom had an interest in working in conjunction with Western medicine. There were now iridologists, kinesiologists, homeopaths and a cognitive psychologist working in the rooms. As the business grew my lack of a business background became more obvious. I needed something more solid than New Age theories to direct me.

Success strategies

Then a patient of mine lent me a series of tapes by a well-known success strategist. At first I was reluctant to listen to them as I thought the presenter's gleaming smile, suit, tie and briefcase represented exactly what I didn't want to become. The content of the tapes didn't sound at all spiritual or New Age either, but within minutes of listening to the first one I recognised its power and its uplifting potential. From then on, I played the tapes whenever I was in my car. Soon I needed more, and I started going to success seminars instead of New Age festivals. I couldn't get enough of seeing national and international speakers present their proven methods for success in life and business.

It was obvious to me that these people, in their own words, 'walked the talk'. They had succeeded in life, they had their act together, and I felt inspired to follow their recommendations. I had always wanted to live life in accord with the philosophy that launched the hippie movement, encapsulated in its catch-cry, 'create your own reality'. Success strategies helped me to really do this by giving me a structure for clarifying my goals and achieving my dreams. I followed the guidelines, business thrived and I was always fully booked in advance. I regularly travelled and worked overseas. I started lecturing in Traditional Chinese Medicine at the largest natural therapy college in the world. I bought a high-performance convertible as a business car, and I met and married my soul-mate. The years flew past in a blur of activity and excitement.

I achieved everything that I had dreamed of when I left college, but I didn't realise it because, following the recom-mendations of the success books and tapes, I focused on constantly setting and achieving new goals. To keep up with this I found myself going faster and faster.

Time became my enemy. From the moment I woke I raced frantically through the day, constantly checking my watch. It is particularly hard to stay on schedule as a therapist because there is an element of unpredictability in each case. The success of the therapy hinges on being able to create trust in the patients. Often this takes a while, and many patients don't open up about their real issues until the final few minutes of their treatment. If a person is in the middle of revealing their deepest fears or hopes, you can hardly show them out when their time is up. This is when they most need your full attention.

On a typical day my first appointment would run five minutes late, the second ten, and so on. By the middle of the

day I would be desperately trying to create time. I remembered a stress management seminar that I had attended in
which the presenter discussed different types of personalities. One of these was the guy who goes to the toilet and
flushes the toilet while still urinating, in the belief that such
actions speed up the process and create more 'time' for other
things. I could relate to that description, and actually caught
myself performing similar actions every now and then.

I enjoyed the heavy work load though, and I enjoyed
being a therapist. This was not only because I could help
others, but also because working on others took away my
own pain. Pain has an energy associated with it. We usually
express this verbally which is why we yelp, scream or cry
when we hurt ourselves. I was specialising in high-energy
Bodywork: in moving and breaking down energy blockages
in the patient. It was hugely demanding, and I learned to use
the energy of my own pain to go into and move the pain of
others. I would see up to eight patients a day, back-to-back,
and spend at least an hour and a half with each. By the time
I got home I was so wrecked and numb I could barely move.
As an anaesthetic, it was as good as heroin.

The 'go, go, go' Liver Yang quality of the success movement
was also hugely attractive to me, because after spending years
feeling lost, empty and tormented by the frustration and
bitterness of depleted Yang energies, every goal I achieved
gave me a drug-like 'rush' of adrenalin.

Eventually, quiet moments started to become uncomfortable for me, and if I paused long enough I would notice that
I was feeling empty or slightly depressed, but I was too busy
to think about the implications of this. When I got to the
point where anything remotely connected to sitting back,
relaxing or reflecting was physically impossible for me to do,

I knew there was something wrong. But the success strategies motivated me to keep pushing forward regardless of how I was feeling, and I just kept moving. It took strong external intervention to force me to change.

THE WALL

I opened my eyes. There was a man standing at the foot of the bed looking down at me. He was wearing some sort of uniform and holding a large plastic box. I had no idea who he was or what he was doing there. Then I saw another person behind him, a woman. She was dressed the same. I had no idea who she was either. It was hard to make any details out. The woman came closer and sat down on the edge of the bed. She was talking to me, but I couldn't understand what she was saying. Something was wrong. Where the hell was I? What was happening?

The man took the box to the other side of the bed. I could no longer see him, but I heard the box opening and then the distinctive crackling sound of plastic. Then someone else came into my field of vision. After a time, I realised it was my wife. Her look of desperate concern made me even more uneasy. A faint thread of awareness started to creep through the fog in my mind, and the room around me began to look more familiar. I was in my bedroom. It was dark except for a bedside lamp and absolutely silent. But what were these people doing here?

Then the woman leant across me and I recognised the ambulance badge on the sleeve of her shirt. Fear gripped my heart. I wanted to say something but I couldn't. Then I realised that I couldn't breathe either. Panic replaced the fear. Had I died? Was this the end? My whole body felt numb, but it was pulsating at the same time. The woman took my hand, 'Squeeze my hand if you can hear me.' This time I understood what she said and I tried to obey her instructions, but my hand wouldn't move. Was I paralysed? Another cold wave of terror crashed over me. She held one of my hands up and pricked a finger with a needle. A bright red bead of blood formed on my skin but I couldn't feel anything, the hand didn't seem to be connected to me. I tried to speak again but my tongue was thick and bloated and it filled my mouth.

I tried to keep air entering my lungs. 'What is your name?' asked the woman. Impulsively I wanted to answer her, but I couldn't think what my name was. The more I tried to grasp it, the more it eluded me. I didn't know who I was! Panic swept over me again. 'Not to worry,' she said. 'We need to get you up and dressed. It looks like you have had a seizure while you were asleep. You have bitten your tongue and it is badly lacerated. We are going to take you to the hospital for some tests.'

Ending up in hospital was a real shock for me. It seemed a surprise to the doctors too. They could offer no explanation of why I, a perfectly healthy man according to their diagnostics, had had a seizure at my age and without any history of it in my family. There was talk of tests for epilepsy but I didn't want an 'answer' from Western medicine. I knew the seizure had been brought on by something else but I still wasn't prepared to look at the real causes.

The doctors told me that it took on average three months to recover from a Grand Mal Seizure and that I would not be able to work or drive for months. I disregarded this information immediately. I had dedicated so much time to consciously improving health, fitness and stamina that I thought that one week was more than enough time for me. To be on the safe side, I gave myself two weeks before returning to work.

RELAPSE

When I started back at my clinic everything went well until I launched into a passionate and complex explanation of organ dysfunction to my first patient. Before I knew it, a feeling of spinning and fainting rushed over me. I was horrified, I couldn't afford a relapse now. This was an important patient and I was eager to provide a professional and insightful service. Panicking, I instantly applied a Tai-chi breathing technique to suppress the symptoms. It seemed to work so I carefully completed the interview and mentally prepared myself for the Bodywork—the more demanding aspect of the therapy.

As soon as I started, the dizziness and nausea intensified so much that I knew I wouldn't be able to keep collapse at bay much longer. But I couldn't just walk out halfway through the session, so I reduced the intensity of my energetic engagement in the hope that it would get me through to the end. But during the final few minutes I realised that I truly couldn't cope and I had to get out of there as quickly as possible.

The patient was lying face down on the massage table, relaxed and unaware of my condition. I managed to tell her, in what I hoped was a calm manner, to see my receptionist for further assistance. As she was new, she would probably assume that this was how I ended all my treatments. Then I left as fast as I could without alarming her. I rushed into the nearest empty treatment room and I just managed to close the door before the ceiling came down on me, my knees buckled and extreme nausea hit me. I couldn't breathe.

Panic forced me to the floor. The nausea increased and vivid images of Jimi Hendrix's death choking on his own vomit filled my mind, taking me to even higher levels of panic.

I lay there with my heart pounding and the nausea washing over me in waves. My mind could make no sense of up or down, left or right. The floor felt like the ceiling, I was spinning in space. I began to think I should call an ambulance or notify my receptionist. Then I realised that I was unable to move, or even call out for help. I was utterly powerless. The room continued to spin, I knew I was on the verge of another seizure and I knew I couldn't let that happen. I focused on doing Tai-chi breathing while remaining in the same position and after a while, a slight easing in my stomach gave me a glimmer of hope. When it became clear that I was through the worst of it, I slowly pulled myself up into a sitting position.

I could hear traffic outside and voices in the reception area. Although I didn't know how long I had been lying there, I realised that the trip into my inner hell had gone unnoticed. I finally managed to stand up and, after slamming into the door with my forehead, I stumbled out of the room to the reception area. The frightened look on my receptionist's face told me that I looked the way I felt. She asked if I was okay, but I could only muster up enough strength to ask her to cancel my appointments for at least one month, before I staggered out the door.

THE ROAD TO REPAIR

Now I had to accept the fact that serious damage had been done and that it would take time and professional help for me to heal properly whether I wanted it to or not. The seizure had resulted from the major imbalance of Yin and Yang that I had created in myself. It physically forced me into months of Yin building because every time I stepped back into work, or Yang mode, dizziness and nausea would overwhelm me and force me to stop. I noticed that the symptoms were worst when my mind was operating at high speed, independent of the body and the external world. This created a separation of body and mind. However, I also discovered that at the onset of the symptoms, if I moved into a simple Tai-chi posture, my breath in conjunction with the Tai-chi movement could bring my mind back to every part of my body, allowing energy to flow again and the symptoms to pass.

Even though I wanted to immediately get back into action territory, where everything about myself that I didn't want to look at could be suppressed, I was literally forced to enter unfamiliar Yin territory. I saw that I was going to have to treat myself the same as I would a patient who came to me in such a state. I had had many patients over the years who had achieved material wealth, success or power but who lacked inner peace and happiness. I had given them strategies for developing Yin: strategies for creating buffer zones before going to work, powerful supplements to fuel their bodies and minds, high-energy Bodywork to break down obstructions in their Energy Fields, and counselling to identify the cause of their emptiness and their need to keep moving.

Funnily enough, even though I had the same symptoms as most of these people—I was an insomniac, I was having panic attacks and was frequently unable to breathe, I was constantly teetering on the verge of collapse—I had never seen any similarity between them and myself until now. I had simply suppressed and ignored everything I was feeling. It made me realise that if material success is not the outcome of balanced Yin and Yang you will never be able to enjoy it.

Like these patients, my recovery would entail serious work on body, mind and spirit. Since I couldn't go to see myself, I looked for other practitioners who would cover all the elements I covered in my own work: counselling, Bodywork, nutrition and so on.

Shiatsu

I began by booking regular weekly treatments with Michie, a Shiatsu practitioner. She had trained in Japan and was an experienced and dedicated worker. I would lie on a futon on the floor in her clinic and she would use the weight of her whole body to apply incredible pressure to points on the body where energy was blocked. It was excruciatingly painful and highly effective. According to Shiatsu diagnostics, on one level the seizure was considered a result of a Spleen so deficient that it was unable to transport Blood to the brain, thus triggering a massive spasm to attempt to rebalance the body.

My lifestyle of constant focus, endless rushing and insomnia was the cause for depleting my Spleen and Blood. You can also have a seizure after taking speed for days on end without stopping, sleeping or allowing yourself to 'come down'. Thinking back, my wife told me that one of the first questions the ambulance officers had asked her was whether I had been taking drugs. It was a bit of a shock to think that my dedication to work had put me in the same place as my drug-taking might once have done.

Medicinal herbs and supplements

Next I went to see a Chinese Herbalist who worked at the college I lectured at. The clinic was set up like a traditional

Chinese apothecary and lined from floor to ceiling with shelves of huge glass jars full of exotic, unidentifiable material including roots, bark and leaves. The smell of Moxa, a strong, aromatic herb used in conjunction with acupuncture, wafted through the air and Chinese flute music played softly in the background. It was all outlandish by Western medical standards but I would often find myself sitting in the waiting room next to pensioners or housewives who flipped through out-dated magazines and found it all completely normal.

According to the diagnostics of Traditional Chinese Medicine, my seizure was associated with a depleted Spleen. That led to phlegm production which interrupted the flow of Chi to the brain. I committed myself to a year of potent Chinese herbs administered on a fortnightly basis.

Wanting to take as holistic an approach as possible, I also sought a Western point of view. I went to a clinical nutritionist and naturopath who analysed my blood, made dietary recommendations and gave me high quality minerals and antioxidants, the benefits of which were perceptible within days. It was this that made me realise just how important vitamins and minerals are for the body to repair or even to operate properly in the first place. Even though I had a 'good' diet and always ate properly, it just wasn't enough. Food doesn't have the nutritional value it once did, and the situation is only going to get worse. I don't think we can be healthy anymore without the correct nutritional supplementation.

As Dr J. Zuess points out in his introduction for a seminal text on nutritional supplements, the standard American diet doesn't provide the levels of nutrition necessary for optimal health and longevity. Not only that, but for some Americans it may not even provide the minimal levels of nutrients necessary for life (Gastelu 2000). In my experience this statement could be applied equally to other Western countries.

The psychic

Leaving no stone unturned, I decided to visit a clairvoyant as well. Someone had been recommended to me many times in the past by patients and friends, but he was usually fully booked months ahead. I decided to phone him anyway. As luck would have it, he had just had a cancellation and was able to see me the following morning. He worked from a boutique hotel and, as my wife was now doing all the driving, we actually arrived early. My wife went off to find some magazines to read and I waited on the far side of the hotel foyer while the receptionist phoned the clairvoyant's room.

A few minutes later the lift doors opened in the corridor behind me and I turned to see a middle-aged man with long, straggling grey hair limping towards me. He had an intense gaze and bright blue eyes. Before I had even had a chance to say anything, he pointed over at my wife who was reading magazines in a chair on the far side of the foyer and said, 'You two have really got a good connection'. He then looked at me directly and said, 'I am worried about your health. You are in bad shape and need to make immediate and dramatic changes to your life or you are going to have more episodes.'

I was really shocked. I had been to many clairvoyants in my time but he was extraordinary. I hadn't said a word, yet he had read the relationship with my wife, although we were nowhere near each other, and he had seen my true state of health even though outwardly I looked fit and healthy. He came closer and shook my hand. I could feel a sensation like butterflies in my stomach from the energy he emitted. My wife joined us and we followed him to the lift and his consulting room on the third floor. For the next hour I sat at a table opposite him while he reeled off the things that had brought me to this point in my life, from unresolved family issues to expending far too much of my own energy on my work. As we left, he gestured to my wife and said, 'You are going to have to talk to her you know'. This seemed a bit cryptic but the entire experience had been so overwhelming that I thought no more of it. I resolved to follow his advice and pay attention foremost to my health.

Homeopathy and counselling

The next step in my recovery was almost accidental. We decided to spend the weekend in the country with Judith, a friend of my wife's who happened to be a homeopath. During our conversations I mentioned my symptoms and she offered to prepare a homoeopathic remedy for the dizziness that I kept experiencing. I casually followed her into her clinic and sat down. Within a few minutes under her gentle but relentless probing, I found myself flooded with memories of a tragic event that had occurred 12 years earlier.

I was stunned by the sudden emergence of these terrible memories and their overwhelming emotional impact, and I tried to keep my tears at bay. As a therapist myself, I realised the relevance and significance of the memories and decided to share them with Judith. In a detached and almost clinical manner I began to describe the event. However, the intensity of the unacknowledged emotional damage sabotaged all attempts at distance and I felt as if I was thrown back into the devastating scene.

It was 11.00 a.m. on a humid spring morning years ago.

I stood in the maternity ward of the hospital holding my newly born, dead, baby son in my arms. He almost looked like me, with the difference that he didn't move and there was no expression on his perfect little face. The delivery room was dreadfully silent. There was no laughter, no joy, no cries of a newborn baby. Their absence struck terror into my heart. One of the nurses burst into tears and ran from the room. I felt that I was in a vacuum, in a nightmarish world where birth and death occurred simultaneously. The midwife asked me if I wanted a photo taken with my son in my arms. I nodded mutely, shell-shocked and unaware of what I was doing. The memory of that photo stayed in my mind but I could never bear to look at it.

It wasn't until I sat in Judith's clinic that I realised that my seizure had taken place on the twelfth anniversary of my baby's death: what was, without doubt, one of the worst days of my life. My relationship with the mother of the baby never recovered and, after the funeral of our son, we had an extremely painful separation and went different ways. We never spoke to each other again, but I heard from mutual friends that for several agonising years afterwards she had tried hard to comprehend and to accept what had happened. I, on the other hand, had pushed the whole experience to the back of my mind. I simply couldn't bear the pain. I spent the three days following the funeral at the pub drinking myself into a stupor, trying to erase the image of his tiny white coffin being lowered into the ground.

Stored and released memories

I was so weakened from the drugs and booze back then that I had nothing to base any feelings on. My organs were just too depleted to effectively process the pain and I couldn't grieve properly. His death was the final trigger for my deep depression in the late 1980s, when all I could think about was killing myself. The alcohol, drugs and social work had taken their toll but it was his death that brought me to my knees. I had had no help afterwards: no counselling, no therapy. This is not a society that wants to see depressed people and I felt I was supposed to just get over it and keep going.

At the time, I tried to make the pain more bearable by convincing myself that the universe had acted in accord with a bigger picture. I told myself that the soul incarnated in the baby sacrificed itself to become the cause of a major change in the life of two other souls who needed to go in different directions in order to find happiness and fulfilment. However, no rationalisation could stop the pain. It was the first thing I thought of every morning for years afterwards.

The fanatical exercise regime that followed was partly spurred by my desire to just keep moving so the pain couldn't catch up with me. Exercise led me to Tai-chi and meditation and eventually the path to self-mastery but, once you are on that path, not only will you steer clear of the things that will take you off path, but everything that you don't want to deal with will emerge. For me, there was no way to progress further without facing my worst fears, my suppressed pain. Ultimately the seizure forced me to do this, to deal with issues and things about myself that I had been studiously avoiding for years.

Before seeing Judith, I had never talked about the death of my baby, not to friends or colleagues or even my wife. This was partly because I didn't know how to speak about it, but also because I felt like a pariah—everyone else seemed normal and happy but I had this terrible, terrible secret that

I carried around with me. I was terrified of unleashing the pain, of losing control; if I started crying maybe I would never stop. To heal properly though I knew I had to talk about it and deal with it. This must have been what the psychic was referring to when he pointedly told me that I would have to 'talk to my wife'.

Spiritual cognitive therapy: mindfulness

So I made an appointment with an associate, Warren, who had worked from a room in my clinic for many years. He was a psychologist who used a form of cognitive therapy he termed 'mindfulness'. He was interested in cutting-edge Energy medicine and he had developed an extraordinary, high-powered technique in which he assisted you to observe the constructs of your own psyche. I would often send patients to him and they all raved about his work. Now it was my turn.

I felt apprehensive as I sat opposite him in a chair in his room. I was dreading having to talk about my baby's death. Time hadn't healed any wounds for me; the pain and grief were as strong as they had been twelve years ago. Warren didn't say anything though. He gazed at me intently with both warmth and compassion. Then he lit a candle and placed it on the table between us. He suggested that I use the candle as a point to focus on. I looked into the flame. I could feel my Energy Field altering. I kept looking at the candle. Suddenly, in my peripheral vision the room dissolved into oscillating lines. I could see Warren out of the corner of my eye, his head was transforming into different shapes at what seemed like the speed of light. I wondered whether it was my mind throwing archetypes at me but Warren interrupted these thoughts by saying, 'Don't go there'.

I focused on the candle again. The centre of the flame became a black void which sucked me into its centre at a dizzying speed, down towards the place where all the raw pain and anguish was stored. The fear of facing what was there was overwhelming and I could feel my palms sweating and my heart racing but, with an occasional word of encouragement from Warren, who seemed to be able to track my progress, I kept going.

Then I hit the centre, a vortex of swirling, roaring blackness and my stomach, lungs and heart convulsed as the grief and anguish consumed me. My throat burned and tears sprang to my eyes. It was as if I was back in that hospital room. Distantly I could hear Warren saying not to engage with the emotions but to release them and move them out. I wanted to give in to it, to lie on the floor and howl and tear at my hair, but I resisted and, using a Tai-chi breathing technique to stabilise myself, I tried to focus on accepting the death of my son while being in a state of freeflow. Instantly I had an incredible sensation of lightness as some of the blackness moved up my spine and dissipated. For a moment I felt elated but then another wave was upon me, dragging me back to the abyss. Warren's voice cut in again, 'Don't get caught up in it, let it move'. I struggled to maintain a state of freeflow but, in the face of what felt like forty years worth of pain condensed into a solid mass, I occasionally faltered and fell into it.

Over the next few sessions, I learned how to acknowledge, accept and dissipate the pain. At that stage the therapy became an incredibly liberating process. It gave me an insight into the true transitory nature of the emotions. Pain didn't have to be a permanent part of me, it didn't have to dictate my behaviour by making me live in fear of it. I had the option to process it and release it, as well as all the other negative emotions stored in my Energy Field. I was in control and I could set myself free. I kept working on this idea in my daily routine and it wasn't long before my whole life became therapy in progress. It was a challenging time for me. I felt physically and emotionally vulnerable as the release of suppressed painful memories merged with the discomfort of the ongoing seizure symptoms, but I knew I had to stay with it and allow healing to unfold at its own pace.

Balancing Yin and Yang

During my recuperation I had to re-train my mind to accept a Yin state in everything that I did, otherwise my symptoms would recur. The years of commitment to success strategy techniques had made me so dominated by Yang energies though, that I had to change even the way I drove.

Prior to the seizure, whenever I got in my car, before I had even started the engine, my mind had already arrived at my destination. Because there was no physical movement though, instead of freeflow I felt obstruction. Consequently my Liver Yang rose to enforce movement and progress: it demanded that I get there immediately, but the reality of city traffic meant that my rising Yang had to deal with obstacles. Because this Yang wasn't balanced by Yin, obstacles of any sort became an intensely emotional experience and road rage was the result. I had reached the stage where I would drive through red lights because I just couldn't bear to stop, to be still. I was so far gone I actually drove through one once with a police car right on my tail. My noticeboard at home was covered with photos of my car taken by red light and speed cameras.

After the seizure, to counter this Yang madness, every time I got in the car I assigned myself a minimum of two minutes just to sit behind the wheel. The idea was to condition my mind to establish a sense of 'waiting' until I felt comfortable with the idea. I repeated the words 'retreat and wait'. I connected these affirmations to Chi-gung breathing techniques until I found myself in a state of 'acceptance with all there is'. Only then would I start the engine, and then I waited another full minute before taking off. While driving, I kept repeating my new mantra of 'retreat and wait'. This process conditioned me to accept time from the perspective of Yin. In this state I could handle the slow traffic—sort of.

Before the seizure, my biggest challenge was the weekend. Whenever I had days off I felt flat and emotionally down. Initially I had accounted for my 'weekend phobia' by thinking that I had been working too hard or treating too many patients, so the days off brought forward residual heaviness released from my Energy therapy. This was partially correct. The nature of my therapeutic work, which involves an energetic exchange with my patients, meant that as well as dealing with my own blockages I had to also process the pain and trauma released by all the people that I had treated.

The significance of this hit home during my rehabilitation, when I read a book about a Daoist Master who had used Energy techniques to heal a dangerously ill patient. The treatment was successful, but it had taken the Master three months in a retreat to recover from the work he did (Deng Ming-Dao 1993). Obviously I was not working on the level of a Daoist Master, but the amount of energy I invested in each patient had steadily been increasing and I had been constantly cutting the time I spent 'cleansing' my Energy Field in between patients as it was 'taking too long'.

Weekends provided a Yin environment to process the release of painful memories, however, I had become so dependent on Yang methods of controlling them, such as weight-lifting, exercise or non-stop work, that I simply couldn't sit back and deal with anything in a mode of 'retreat and wait'. The seizure forced me to learn to do this; I now had to process major physical and emotional trauma without relying on Yang energies. The doctors were wrong—it didn't take me three months to recover, it took me years.

Everything changed after the seizure; I sold my business and moved into a new phase of research and writing. Change is always difficult and at times I thought it was the end of the world, but it allowed me to finally let go of my obsession with achieving goals at the cost of all else, to understand the importance of a balanced lifestyle and to face my fears and internal demons. I came out of it a much happier and healthier person.

CHAPTER NINE

Building body, mind and spirit

INNER ENERGY CRISIS

In the West, most people do not realise that everything we do costs energy and that we don't have an unlimited supply. If we don't make an effort to conserve and build our energy by living, thinking and acting in a manner that is beneficial to us, our energy stores will be drained. Then we can become emotionally weak, vulnerable and reactive and life can spiral downwards into negativity and ill health.

I set off a downward cycle in my own life several times by taking drugs, by not dealing with my own pain and then by over-work. These were internal and arguably self-generated causes but, based on my years of experience as a therapist, I believe that every one of us can reach this point via one means or another. Scores of my patients who had never taken drugs or burned-out at work ended up in the same place due to factors beyond their control. These included family dramas, the death of a loved one, divorce, accidents and even natural disasters. The internal imbalances that arise from the pain and trauma of these external factors can be just as destructive as those derived from an inappropriate lifestyle.

However, if you live in a way that conserves and builds your energy, it can correct existing imbalances and create a base from which you will be able to respond to future traumatic events. Further, it will do so in a manner that will limit the development of blockages in your Energy Field and prevent a downward spiral starting. This kind of lifestyle is based on routine and includes exercise, meditation, Chi-training, goal setting, a healthy diet, nutritional supplements, therapy, and beneficial sexual practices.

DEALING WITH DISCOMFORT

Your health and wellbeing are critically important. If you make a commitment to developing and improving yourself it will automatically improve everything in your life. It sounds simple enough, but the important things are never easy to do and improving your health and wellbeing will bring you face to face with discomfort. No one likes discomfort, and much of our Western lifestyle is actually based on avoiding it at all costs, but discomfort is a part of life—no matter how sophisticated we become this will not change. The trick is to master the discomfort yourself. In the long term, facing the discomfort of getting up early, of learning to eat well or of exercising routinely is much easier and of much greater benefit than dealing with the more serious discomfort that will inevitably arise if you don't.

GET RHYTHM

If you want to feel great it is important to establish rhythm and routine in your life. This provides a stable framework for development. Many people tell me that they believe it's better to live 'spontaneously' than by routine. This is because, like most of us, they have lost their relationship with natural rhythms and replaced them with bad habits. These range from the physical, such as staring at a computer screen until 2:00 a.m. and drinking coffee and eating chocolate to stay awake night after night, to the psychological, like refusing to take responsibility for the self.

True spontaneity arises from healthy organs, and the only way to get healthy organs is through routine and rhythm. Traditional Chinese Medicine has established that Chi moves through the twelve organs and five elements in a regular cycle. To build health, happiness and success you need to live in harmony with this cycle.

Each morning, when the Chi is in the Metal and Earth element, you have a window of opportunity to start changing your life. Metal is about embracing the new by letting go of old conditioning and Earth is about operating as an independent individual by building Chi and Blood.

Time	Organ	Element
3:00 a.m.—5:00 a.m.	Lungs	Metal Element
5:00 a.m.—7:00 a.m.	Large Intestine	Metal Element
7:00 a.m.—9:00 a.m.	Stomach	Earth Element
9:00 a.m.—11:00 a.m.	Spleen	Earth Element
11:00 a.m.—1:00 p.m.	Heart	Fire Element
1:00 p.m.—3:00 p.m.	Small Intestine	Fire Element
3:00 p.m.—5:00 p.m.	Bladder	Water Element
5:00 p.m.—7:00 p.m.	Kidney	Water Element
7:00 p.m.—9:00 p.m.	Pericardium	Fire Element
9:00 p.m.—11:00 p.m.	San Jiao (Triple Heater)	Fire Element
11:00 p.m.—1:00 a.m.	Gall Bladder	Wood Element
1:00 a.m.—3:00 a.m.	Liver	Wood Element

So, depending on what you do between 5:00 and 9:00 a.m., you can either shape the day ahead and your destiny, or let others shape your life for you in accord with their needs. To shape your day yourself and create your own reality, you need to do a body-mind-spirit workout during the Metal element and Large Intestine time (5:00—7:00 a.m.) and then have a Chi and Blood building breakfast during the Earth element and Stomach time (7:00—9:00 a.m.).

Doing your body-mind-spirit workout when the Chi is in the Metal element and eating the right breakfast at Stomach time sets in place a chain of positive interactions within the five element cycle. Earth nurtures Metal (control), Metal nurtures Water (Jing), Water nurtures Wood (happiness), Wood nurtures Fire (joy) and Fire nurtures Earth (independence).

Interestingly, modern sports science also identifies the morning as the best and most effective time to work out, as exercising early raises the metabolic rate for up to fifteen hours to follow.

For people who are unable to do a workout at that time in the morning, I would recommend trying to establish a routine that works with your life. Get up at a regular time, drink water and stretch. Find time for the rest of the body–mind–spirit workout during the day or in the evening. Even if you feel exhausted beforehand, it will build your energy and revitalise you. This will benefit everyone around you as well.

THE BODY–MIND–SPIRIT WORKOUT

This workout includes elements of Eastern practices such as Tai-chi, Chi-gung or yoga, because there are no equivalent Western practices for this kind of inner energy work, as well as Western exercises. Thus the body–mind–spirit workout fuses the 'internal' practices of the East with the 'external' practices of the West.

While I recognise that these Eastern practices already cover full body–mind–spirit development, I have found that many of my patients and students resist some elements of the discipline, so they are not able to gain the full benefits of the practice. This workout is designed for the body–mind constitution of the West. It particularly targets deficiencies, blockages and stress, three major health concerns in current Western societies.

Step 1: 10 min   Get up, drink water
Step 2: 15 min   Stretch

Step 3: 30 min   Meditate
Steps 4-6: 60 min   Chi-training, endurance and weights
Step 7: 5 min   Focus your energy

Total: 2 hours a day to build health and happiness

Step one: Getting up

Regular early morning rising is the first step in the body–mind–spirit workout. It sounds simple, but these days most people wake up feeling tired. There are many reasons for this, including emotional and physical stress, poor diet, eating on the run and use of alcohol or drugs or both. As these things all obstruct and deplete the Chi, it can't deliver that instant 'awake' feeling. Staying in bed and getting more sleep seems like the solution. However, extra sleep doesn't guarantee increased energy or lead to a more positive attitude towards getting up. In fact, sleeping in can make the situation worse and leave you feeling worse when you finally do get up. This is because sleeping in won't move blocked Chi.

When you get up, immediately drink filtered water at room temperature. During sleep, the body has been deprived of water. So drinking water kick-starts your system, flushes out the 'debris' (this is the time for a bowel motion) and pre-pares the body to 'receive the new'. If you get up and get into your daily activities without drinking water first, don't be surprised if you feel dry, stuck and rigid. I drink two litres, but it is best to start by drinking an amount that is comfortable for you, maybe a couple of glasses.

Most people feel grumpy in the morning. This is partly because the Liver Chi is not flowing yet, but also because this is a vulnerable time. Emotional issues are close to the surface, which is why people who are depressed are reminded most strongly of their condition in the few minutes after waking. Everyone has some degree of what I call the 'doubt factor' operating as well: a busy day ahead, new professional directions or stress about personal issues, which also makes them reluctant to get out of bed. The trick is to just get up and get going. It becomes a habit after a while and the body becomes conditioned to feel 'ready to rise' as soon as you wake up.

Step two: Stretch

You need to stretch your body before engaging in other activities. Stretching makes the Chi flow, and this reduces your 'doubt factor' significantly. The Liver Chi, in particular, needs to flow freely in order to open the eyes, to soften the muscles, to lubricate the joints and tendons and to generate a good mood. If the Liver Chi is obstructed, the eyes open slowly in the morning, and the body aches and feels stiff and tight because the tendons and joints aren't lubricated and the muscles are rigid. Stretching always feels difficult at first, but the more you stretch the easier it becomes.

If you don't know any stretches I would suggest a session with a personal trainer. A personalised set of stretches can also help to counteract any regular stresses you place on your body.

Step three: Meditate

So, now you are up, the water-drinking routine has initiated the 'letting go' phase, the stretching has begun to make your Chi flow, and you are ready to 'receive the new'. This is the best time for meditation. There are numerous philosophies on meditation and people are always asking me which is the best type to do. Fortunately, I believe that there is a universal system underlying all meditative techniques, and that each practice connects you to the Divine source in its own way. In other words, do whichever one you prefer, but make sure that it is a true meditation practice, and not simply relaxation.

I find that many people confuse meditation with relaxation techniques. But they are distinctly different. Relaxation techniques, such as calming your breathing, imagining that you are in a beautiful peaceful environment and so on, encourage an alignment of the conscious and sub-conscious mind which generates a calm state. This is relaxation.

Meditation, however, results from an alignment of the conscious and sub-conscious mind, and the super-consciousness or the mind of God. This you can't learn from a book. You need to 'receive' it by meditating in the presence of, or under the guidance of, someone who has been initiated by a spiritual master and has then undergone training to do the same for others.

In a deep meditative state the electrical activity of the brain slows down, moving progressively from the beta state of normal life, to the alpha waves of relaxation, down to the theta and delta waves that dominate our creativity and healing sleep. The lower the brainwaves, the more dominant the Yin becomes and the more the meditation can counter the uncontrolled or pathological Yang energies that result from an intense, high-stress lifestyle.

Meditating allows you to fill your body, mind and spirit with a tangible experience of perfection, inner peace or unconditional love. Although many people find it hard to establish a regular meditation practice, the benefits are profound. It provides a source of joy and bliss for the rest of the day and enables you to feel good about yourself and life in general.

To carry this bliss into the rest of your day though, you need to align your body with your meditation experience. If you go straight into your everyday tasks without integrating the meditative state with physical reality, the first obstacle you meet, whether it's traffic or a difficult phone call, will jolt you from bliss to stress; from effortlessness to effort; from acceptance to resistance. Following meditation with Chi-training maximises the benefit of the meditation.

Step four: Chi-training

Chi-training is about learning to regulate the flow of Chi—through yoga, Chi-gung, Tai-chi or other internal martial art forms. These teach how to convert obstructions into freeflow and bring the mind back into the body. Daily Chi-training also prevents further obstructions from forming, by enabling you to deal with the Chiblockers: the bullying boss, the people who drain your energy, the traffic, or whatever challenges you, before your organs sustain any damage.

By doing some form of Chi-training after meditating, you learn to superimpose freeflow over blockages and thus you can deal with many more obstacles in your life before you start resisting and reacting to them. This is a key to health, longevity and happiness. If you have never meditated or done Chi-training before, I suggest that you start steps three and four as close together as possible to ensure that you feel their benefits quickly.

To further accelerate your progress towards health and happiness, follow your Chi-training with therapeutic endurance exercise.

Step five: Therapeutic endurance exercise

According to Eastern philosophies a lot of your karma is stored in the legs and hips. This is why many traditional meditation postures, such as the Lotus posture, are so uncomfortable: they facilitate breaking down energy blockages in these areas during meditation. In this body–mind–spirit workout, you can transform the blockages and associated karma through endurance training. But don't expect this transformation to occur every time you jump on a treadmill; you need to do the first four steps of the workout to prepare your body, mind and spirit.

Therapeutic endurance training can be any repetitive activity that brings the heart rate up for a prolonged period, such as cycling, swimming or running. Most people do goal-oriented endurance exercise, aiming for certain times, distances or weight loss, or they exercise with their minds full of deadlines and appointments and use the exercise as a means of stress release. They start exercising and wait for the endorphin release to put them into the 'zone', which empties their heads.

In therapeutically orientated endurance exercise we empty our heads first and then go into the exercise. The idea is to allow the repetition and monotony of the movement to release blockages in your Energy Field. This will also release the negative emotions that were stored in the blockage. As you gain mastery of resistance and acceptance from your Chi-training, you can transform these emotions through acceptance and positive thinking. Thus endurance exercise contributes to spiritual growth as well as physical health. It allows you to strengthen the 'will' which is needed to most effectively utilise the freeflow experience gained from both meditation and Chi-training.

Step six: Therapeutic weight training

Weight training is an important component of the body–mind–spirit workout. However, many people have been put off weight training because they associate it with a sub-culture of unhealthy, narcissistic body-building.

Weight training is based on a cycle of destruction and creation. Existing muscle is destroyed through the training and replaced by stronger, more capable muscle during recovery. From the perspective of Body–Mind medicine, emotions are stored in the muscles. Therefore you can use weight training therapeutically to take your emotions and muscles through this cycle of destruction and creation together. As muscle is destroyed emotional weakness is destroyed along with it, and as muscle is recreated so is emotional strength and wellbeing. You transform weakness into strength. Working therapeutically is not about *forcing* yourself through pain barriers in pursuit of external goals; it's about *flowing* through them to achieve your internal goals.

Weight training is complex though, and if done incorrectly it can be draining and damaging to the body. If you are new to it, I would recommend seeking advice from a qualified trainer. You don't have to go to a gym: I use what is around me and my own body weight. I do push-ups, chin-ups in trees, dips between garbage bins, sit-ups and one-leg squats. In my 'two-day split' program I train chest, shoulders, triceps and abdominal muscles on Mondays and Thursdays and biceps, back and leg muscles on Tuesdays and Fridays. This gives me a recovery period of 72 to 96 hours for each muscle group. I don't recommend doing weights every day: recovery time and training are equally important.

As regular therapeutic weight training is beneficial to the Earth element, it is particularly good for people who are scattered thinkers, who start too many things at once and never finish anything. It is a very reliable way to get back into the body and into control of life. If you are feeling ungrounded, I highly recommend it. No medication can match it—the results are absolutely astonishing.

Step seven: Focus your energy for the day

A Chinese proverb says, 'We are like a piece of wood that needs to be carved every morning. If we don't carve ourselves, someone else will do it for us'. If you want to create success and follow your dreams you need to 'carve yourself', otherwise your path will be directed by external conditions or other people's needs.

If you have done steps one to six, you are well on the path to 'carving yourself'. You have faced and overcome discomfort and resistance and converted your weaknesses into strength. Now is the time to spend five minutes clearly articulating—either verbally or in writing—your goals, because now every word will resonate with body, mind and spirit and the universe will respond accordingly. You will be able to make your dreams reality.

Of course, you can't realise your dreams unless you know what they are. As a therapist I have observed that most people don't really know what they want in life. This is often because obstructions in their Energy Fields have obscured their true selves and their soul's purpose. The body–mind–spirit workout is designed to constantly reduce these obstructions, allowing more of the real you to emerge. So by committing yourself to the workout and then setting achievable goals that focus the energy you have built each day, your soul's purpose will become more and more clear.

One step at a time

This body–mind–spirit workout is designed to allow you to shape your destiny. It may initially appear overwhelming, but relax—I don't recommend launching into everything immediately! The more depleted you are, the more difficult it will be to even get out of bed, so take it step by step. Even if you only adopt step one and repeat that for months, it is still an achievement. The main goal is to continue doing it: to make it a habit. It is better to progress slowly and surely than to try to do too much at once and then give it all up after a couple of weeks.

The idea is to begin gradually and add more when you are able. Initially just try to get up a little earlier each day, drink water and do a few stretches. Go for a short walk if you don't feel up to anything else. While you develop these habits, start eating three nutritious meals a day and take good quality supplements. As your nutritional input improves and organ function starts to improve, your mood will gradually improve too. Your energy levels will increase and the desire to be healthier will increase too. After a while you will be ready to take on more of the body–mind–spirit workout.

FOOD AS FUEL

You are not off the hook yet! There is no point doing all of the above if you are not going to eat properly. None of us would try to drive our cars without petrol, but most people think nothing of trying to run their bodies on either no fuel, or fuel that is so hopelessly contaminated that it will destroy the engine. Over the years I have seen thousands of patients, with every symptom imaginable. An underlying contributing factor in every single case was poor nutrient intake due to eating inappropriately. Food has a direct impact on your wellbeing.

Gateway foods

Based on my own case studies, I have identified a contemporary 'gateway food cycle', which operates on the same premise as 'gateway drugs'—eating 'junk' foods that have little nutritional value leads to a progressive depletion of organ functions and the desire for more junk foods. We all know plenty of people who will, for example, eat a chocolate bar if they are feeling a bit down. Their sugar levels then increase dramatically, creating a mild version of freeflow. However, if you constantly have a high level of sugar in your diet, the organs, particularly the Spleen, will eventually sustain damage leading to a decline in energy. You will then need more sugar to get a 'lift'.

This is the same 'higher and higher' path that many drug users take, and I believe that, via one substance or another—sugar, fat, salt, caffeine, whatever—most of us are currently on an 'organ-damaging instant-gratification trip' that will inevitably lead towards depletion, ill health and depression. Sugar in particular is now being so seriously abused that I think one day future generations will be horrified by the amount of sugar that our children had, just as we are shocked by the amount of opium that children were routinely given in the latter half of the 19th century for ailments, as treats or just to keep them quiet (Carnwath & Smith 2002, p. 6).

Just as designer drugs emerge to cater to the drug market, there are designer snack foods saturated in fat, sugar and flavour enhancers to cater to the junk food market, and a huge proportion of the population is using them. If you want to assess your own levels of 'designer food' dependency, abstain from all foods containing high levels of sugar, salt, fat, artificial flavouring or caffeine for a week. After just a few days you will experience an emotional instability that may surprise and shock you.

☯ CASE STUDY: GATEWAY FOODS

I had a patient, Anita, who became trapped in the gateway food cycle. She had constant cravings and nothing ever satisfied her. Her breakfast would usually be white toast, butter and jam. This translates as refined flour, fat and sugar: the worst possible breakfast food combination in my opinion! By 10:00 a.m. she would be craving something again, and would eat cake or biscuits: more refined flour, fat and sugar. Lunch was usually take-away food, but immediately afterwards she would need to eat something sweet.

If you crave something sweet after you have eaten a meal, it is more than likely because the food you have eaten has created an imbalance because it was too fatty or a poor combination of ingredients. This generates a distortion in the Energy Field and you instinctively seek a way of moving Chi again. Sugar will create this impression. But if you eat a nutrient-poor meal and then follow it with a sweet desert you are just entrenching your problems.

Anita's sugar, fat and salt 'addiction' kept eroding her energy; she ended up snacking constantly but never felt satisfied. She became obese and developed Spleen problems including lack of focus, fatigue and emotional reactivity. This had a negative effect on every aspect of her life. It took a long time for her to break this pattern of constant dissatisfaction and constant craving. What the body is craving is nutrients, but you can't recognise this when you are trapped in the cycle.

I immediately gave her powerful nutritional supplements and suggested substitute foods. She had tried all sorts of crash diets but I approached the case as I would a drug addiction. There is no point just giving things up, you need to replace things and change your direction and focus. For example, step one for Anita was to replace her morning toast and jam with porridge and honey. This satisfied her desire for something sweet, but also meant she could last up to four hours before getting the feeling of 'needing something' again. Bit by bit we whittled away at her habits, adding nutrients, replacing types of snacks, and then adding in some light exercise and other things that would help develop her sense of wellbeing. To her surprise, even though she was not eating less, she eventually achieved her ideal weight, she developed a healthy glow in her skin and her eyes looked clearer.

FOOD—WHEN, HOW AND WHY

The food you consume has a direct effect on your ability to function, to absorb and process information. Substances that deplete the Yin, such as junk foods, sugar or drugs make people less productive, because with insufficient Yin the mind lacks the necessary structure, boundaries and control to allow it to operate effectively. Ideally, you should consume foods that will enhance your concentration, attention and memory function. Foods that nourish rather than deplete the Spleen are the most important for this, as the Spleen is the prime organ responsible for mental function. Foods that enhance the function of the Spleen ensure an effective, energetic and productive day.

Diet is a complex area, and the 'best' foods for each person vary depending on constitution, state of health, lifestyle, etc. However, following the suggestions below should improve most people's health but I would recommend seeking advice from a nutrition professional.

Breakfast

Breakfast is a crucial meal which should be consumed between 7:00 and 9:00 a.m. when the Chi is in the Stomach. Later than this is not beneficial, because from 9:00 to 11:00 a.m. the Chi is in the Spleen. If you haven't eaten a proper breakfast by then the Spleen, which has to provide you with Chi for the rest of the day, has nothing to draw on. It will be forced to draw from your Jing instead and we all know by now where that is going to lead.

I recommend long-chain sugars such as porridge or congee for breakfast. Have some high-quality protein as well. This is particularly important if you are doing the full body–mind–spirit workout. My breakfast is a protein shake followed by porridge made from organic oats. I avoid fat, sugar, white flour products and highly-processed breakfast cereals. If you want to eat toast, make it from a nutritious bread and have honey instead of jam. Sit down to eat your breakfast in a calm environment.

Lunch

Between 11:00 a.m. and 1:00 p.m. the Chi is in the Heart, and between 1:00 and 3:00 p.m. the Chi is in the Small Intestine. I would recommend eating lunch between 12:00 and 1:30 p.m. This is when Yang peaks, so it is the best time to eat your main meal, with your main protein intake for the day, as protein requires Yang to digest. Because this is Heart time it is also important to eat with joy. Eating lunch under stress (like at your desk at work) affects the Heart adversely. Then the imbalances of the Heart such as anxiety, insomnia, depression and an unsettled and restless mind will begin to develop.

Food that is cooked and warm is ideal for lunch. From my experience, a beneficial lunch would be a combination of rice, which nourishes and nurtures the Spleen (white rice is preferable as many people cannot digest brown rice properly), protein such as lamb, beef, chicken, fish or beans and a good serve of vegetables. As a rule of thumb, green and orange vegetables are always good. Asian-style meals often have the perfect combination of these elements.

I avoid foods that contain cheese and large amounts of fat, or cold and raw foods as they are taxing to the Spleen. I also do not eat pasta and sandwiches at lunchtime, as wheat has a high concentration of an amino acid which is used to treat insomnia, so if you eat wheat products it is best to do so in the evening. If you have foods such as pizza or cheesy, creamy pasta for lunch, I can guarantee that your ability to focus and concentrate in the afternoon will be impaired. You will be tired, have a short attention span and will feel unproductive.

If you suffer from energy lows in the afternoons and need a 'sweet' snack, I would recommend seasonal fruits or dried fruits and nuts.

Evening meal

If you have eaten a good breakfast and lunch at the right times, the timing of your evening meal is not as important. The main thing is that you should finish eating at least two hours before you go to sleep.

The evening is Yin time, so you need to eat a Yin-nurturing meal. This means eating light foods that are easy to digest, rather than fatty foods or even the lunch recommended above, with its protein that requires Yang to digest. If you eat a heavy meal like that in the evening, your body uses the energy that is required for a deep, nurturing sleep to digest the food instead. This can contribute to the development of sleeping disorders. I have successfully treated numerous cases of insomnia simply by asking the patient to reverse their lunch and dinner menus.

If you want to cook an evening meal, it need be no more than steamed rice and vegetables, otherwise wholesome bread and salad would be good. This approach to eating is in harmony with the 24-hour Chi cycle so it will build energy and health, but it does entail changing your main meal from dinner to lunch. This may take a while to implement and get used to, but after a few weeks you will definitely notice the benefit.

Changing your own habits, your family's habits, and cultural habits can be very challenging. Start by adding supplements as they will immediately impact upon cravings which reflect nutrient depletion, and then perhaps target breakfast. Take it one step at a time.

NUTRITIONAL SUPPLEMENTS

Lifestyle factors of the 21st century constantly deplete our energy. I believe that even with a perfect diet, we cannot counter all these adverse elements any more without help. In his exhaustive analysis of the nutritional supplements, Daniel Gastelu lists the reasons to take supplements. These include making up for the poor nutrient content of many foods we eat; and replacing nutrients destroyed in foods by cooking and in the body by smoking, alcohol consumption, drug use, and pollution (Gastelu 2000, p. 9).

Supplements establish what therapists call 'nutrient saturation' and replenish the whole system. They help re-establish correct organ function, which generates emotional balance and mental clarity. Preventative medicine is the way of the future and supplementation is a crucial element of preventative medicine and anti-ageing. However, you have to use an effective product and it needs to be managed by a professional. Billions of dollars are being spent each year on herbal or nutritional products but the majority of people self-prescribe, and sadly, in most cases this is ineffective and can even be dangerous.

Many people, for example, are now taking formulas containing ginseng and guarana to try to increase their energy. However, these herbs are Yang builders and if you take them when you really need to build Yin they can cause unpleasant effects such as aggression and a feeling of being 'wound-up'. I would recommend seeking ongoing professional advice from a nutritionist, naturopath or other qualified person to ensure your supplements are effective and administered in response to your changing state of health.

DON'T WASTE YOUR JING

The substance which determines your basic constitutional strength and vitality is Jing. The more Jing you have the better you are able to feel. Accordingly, Jing is supposed to be carefully managed. So plan not only to build Jing but also to conserve it. Many of the things that use up our stores of Jing are fairly obviously unhealthy—drugs, cigarettes, booze, junk foods and so on—but there are other, less obvious things we do that waste Jing. Prominent amongst these are inappropriate sexual practices.

Sex and Jing

In learning to build and manage our Chi and Jing, we also need to understand the energetic laws associated with sex. In Traditional Chinese Medicine, sex is viewed as an integral part of health, as it has a direct impact on your levels of Jing. If you don't apply intelligence to your sex life, in terms of when and how often, after a while your Chi and Jing will become depleted and you will experience the resulting deficiencies and pathologies.

The mornings are for building Chi and setting the ground for a productive day ahead. Having sex in the morning interferes with this. If you wake up feeling tired, as most of us do, and then have sex (this includes masturbation), you may feel temporarily uplifted but half an hour later you will have even less energy than before and less ability to focus. Hence you will miss the morning's window of opportunity to shape the day and your destiny. I consider early evening (when the Chi is in the Kidneys) as the best time to have sex.

It is also important to control how often you have sex, particularly for men, as too-frequent ejaculation can contribute to Jing depletion and impotence. TCM principles recommend an optimum ejaculation rate based on your age and state of health. Following these recommendations will contribute to a healthier and longer life. For example, if you are in your teens and twenties, generally speaking, ejaculation once a day is okay. In your thirties, if your health is average, once every other day. In your forties and fifties, I wouldn't recommend ejaculating more than three times a week.

In women the orgasm is considered to be the equivalent of ejaculation in men, but the loss of Jing in female orgasm is much less than the loss experienced in male ejaculation. In terms of building Chi however, it is still important for women to regulate the rate at which they orgasm.

Yin and Yang and sex

Controlling ejaculation rates can prove challenging for many men, particularly those who have high Yang levels, but once they learn how, not only will they be more healthy, but paradoxically they will be able to have a more deeply fulfilling sex life. Sexual energies are always of a Yang nature, as they associate with action rather than passivity. As men are Yang, sexual arousal for them is 'Yang on Yang'—a 'double Yang' state in which 'advance and act' dictates behaviour. This creates a powerful primal urge and in this state action is all that matters. There is no sense of having 'time' or the frame of mind to incorporate all emotionality, so deeper orgasmic experiences are not possible.

Balancing Yang with Yin qualities is important for a harmonious sex life. If the man does not learn to transcend his

Yang during arousal, sex is not satisfying for the woman and over time it can lead to her withdrawal. In terms of physical health, this balance is also important because in males, 'double Yang' sex consumes more Jing than sex that climaxes with a deep and fulfilling orgasm. As Jing is the foundation for sexual power, constant 'double Yang' sex depletes the Jing and prepares the ground for future sexual problems and dysfunction.

Women are Yin and, as such, are better placed than men to have deeply satisfying sexual experiences. When women become sexually aroused and experience the Yang desire for action, it is automatically tempered by Yin. Accordingly, they can integrate a Yang desire for 'fast and forceful' with the Yin quality of 'slow and gentle'. In addition, well-developed Yin qualities give a sense of 'time' in which you can make choices and become fully integrated with every aspect of your mind and body. When this happens Chi flows evenly and freely through every meridian, affecting every organ and every emotion and creating a profound feeling of bliss.

THERAPY

All of the factors above—the exercise, the good diet, supplements, and beneficial sex—are the equivalent of putting fuel, water and oil into your car, and, like cars, I believe we also need regular maintenance. This is where therapeutic input comes into the picture. I would recommend regular Bodywork, Shiatsu, acupuncture, homeopathy, naturopathy, counselling or any other treatment that breaks down the blockages in your body and keeps the Chi flowing. Ongoing therapy is particularly important if you are very depleted or depressed.

HIGHER AND HIGHER

It is human nature to always go for the better high, and the path of body-mind-spirit development delivers much more exciting and rewarding results than chasing external goals or unsustainable highs. Once you have experienced the exhilarating thrill of generating freeflow yourself, you will naturally begin to avoid the things that create blockages— whether it be drugs, junk foods or something more subtle. You will find yourself drawn instead to the things that keep Chi flowing, the practices that develop and integrate body, mind and spirit. Once you start progressing along that path you will instinctively recognise it as being fundamentally 'right'. This is because the Human Energy Field is linked with the Universal Energy Field, or the mind of God, and living in harmony with universal laws is the path to the ultimate high.

THE BEGINNING

Bibliography

BOOKS

Booth, M. 2003, *Cannabis: A history*, Transworld Publishers, London.

Breggin, P. 2001, *The Antidepressant Fact Book*, Perseus Publishing, Cambridge.

Carnwath, T. & Smith, I. 2002, *Heroin Century*, Routledge, London.

Huang, Al Chuanling. 1987, *Embracing Tiger Return to Mountain*, Celestial Arts, Berkeley, CA.

Crane, G. 2000, *Bones of the Master*, Bantam Press, New York, London.

Deng, Ming-Dao. 1993, *Chronicles of Tao*, HarperSanFrancisco, San Francisco.

Gastelu, D. 2000, *The Complete Nutritional Supplements Buyer's Guide*, Three Rivers Press, New York.

Grinspoon, L. 1971, *Marijuana Reconsidered*, Harvard University Press, Cambridge.

Heller, J., Henkin, W.A. 1991, *Bodywise*, North Atlantic Books, Berkeley, CA.

Hammer, L. 1991, *Dragon Rises, Red Bird Flies*, Station Hill Press, Barrytown, NY.

Kaptchuk, T. 1990, *Chinese Medicine: The Web that has no Weaver*, Rider, London.

Larre, C., Rochat de la Vallée, E. 1996, *The Seven Emotions*, Monkey Press, Cambridge, London.

Maciocia, G. 1989, *The Foundations of Chinese Medicine*, Churchill Livingstone, Edinburgh, New York.

Maoshing, Ni. 1996, *The Eight Treasures: Energy Enhancement Exercise*, SevenStar Communications, Santa Monica, CA.

Nahas, G. 1973, *Marihuana: Deceptive Weed*, Raven Press, New York.

Oschman, J. 2000, *Energy Medicine: the Scientific Basis of Bioenergy Therapies*, Harcourt Brace/Churchill Livingstone, Edinburgh.

Oschman, J. 2003, *Energy Medicine in Therapeutics and Human Performance*, Butterworth Heinemann, Amsterdam, Boston.

Pinchbeck, D. 2002, *Breaking Open the Head: A Psychedelic Journey into the Heart of Contemporary Shamanism*, Broadway Books, New York.

Ross, J. 1985, *The Organ Systems of Traditional Chinese Medicine*, Churchill Livingstone, Edinburgh, New York.

Singh, K. 2002, *Vibrant Celestial Meditation*, National Book Organisation & The World Spiritual Foundation, New Delhi.

Sankey, M. 1999, *Esoteric Acupuncture*, Mountain Castle Publishing, Inglewood, CA.

Sheldrake, R. 1991, *The Rebirth of Nature: The Greening of Science and God*, Park Street Press, Rochester, Vermont.

Strassman, R. 2001, *DMT: The Spirit Molecule*, Park Street Press, Rochester, Vermont.

Streatfeild, D, 2001, *Cocaine: A Definitive History*, Virgin Books, London.

Su Wen. 1972, *The Yellow Emperor's Classic of Internal Medicine,* (trans Ilza Veith) University of California Press, Berkeley, CA.

Thomas, G. 2002, *This is ecstasy,* Sanctuary House, London.

Walsh, R. 1999, *Essential Spirituality,* John Wiley, New York.

Liao, Waysun. 1990, *Tai chi Classics,* Shambhala Publications, Boston.

Wile, D. 1983, *Tai chi Touchstones: Yang Family Secret Transmissions,* Sweet Ch'i Press, Brooklyn, NY.

ARTICLES/REVIEWS

Avants, S.K., Marcotte, D., Arnold, R., & Margolin, A. 2003, 'Spiritual beliefs, world assumptions and HIV risk behaviour among heroin and cocaine users', *Psychology of Addictive Behaviours,* vol. 17(2), pp. 159–162.

Anglin, D., Burke, C., Perrochet, B., Stamper, E., & Dawud-Noursi, S. 2000, 'History of the methamphetamine problem', *Journal of Psychoactive Drugs,* vol. 32(2), pp. 137–8.

Kaesuk Yoon, C. 2004, 'The missing drink' quote from Dr Robert Dudley, University of California, Berkeley, *Sydney Morning Herald,* March 27–28, p. 32.

Frishman, W., Del Vecchio, A., Sanal, S., & Ismail, A. 2003, 'Cardiovascular manifestations of substance abuse Pt 2: alcohol, amphetamines, heroin, cannabis, and caffeine', *Heart Disease: A Journal of Cardiovascular Medicine,* vol. 5(4), pp. 253–271.

George, H.A. 2002, 'The rave scene and club drugs: Ecstasy', *Nursing News,* vol. 26(4), p. 9.

Hollister, L.E. 1986, 'Health aspects of cannabis', *Pharmacology Review* vol. 38, pp. 1–32.

MacInnes, N., Handley, S.L., & Harding, G.F. 2001, 'Former chronic methylenedioxymethamphetamine (MDMA or ecstasy) users report mild depressive symptoms', *Journal of Psychopharmacology*, Oxford, England, vol. 15(3), pp. 181-6.

Mathias, R., Zickler, P. 2001, 'NIDA conference highlights scientific findings on MDMA/ecstasy', *NIDA—Notes*, vol. 16(5), pp. 1, 5-8, 12.

Mohs, M.E., Watson, R.R., & Leonard-Green, T. 1990, 'Nutritional effects of marijuana, heroin, cocaine, and nicotine', *Journal of the American Dietetic Association*, vol. 90(9), p. 1261.

Parenti, C. 2005, 'Diary' *London Review of Books*, 20 Jan, pp. 30-1.

Parrott, A.C., Buchanan, T., Scholey, A.B., Heffernan, T., & Rodgers, J. 2002, 'Ecstasy/MDMA attributed problems by novice, moderate and heavy recreational users', *Human Psychopharmacology*, vol. 17(6), pp. 309-312.

Resnick, J. 2001, 'The therapeutics of ecstasy', *Psychotherapy in Australia*, vol. 7(4), p. 45.

Sarafin, T.A., Magallanes, J.A.M., Shau, H., Tashkin, D., & Roth, M.D. 1999, 'Oxidative stress produced by marijuana smoke: an adverse effect enhanced by cannabinoids', *American Journal of Respiratory Cell and Molecular Biology*, vol. 20, p. 1287.

Smith, D.J. 2004, 'Spoilt rotten', *The Weekend Australian Magazine*, May 15-16, pp. 13-16.

Swift, W., Hall, W., & Copeland, J. 1998, 'Characteristics of long-term cannabis users in Sydney, Australia', *European Addiction Research*, vol. 4(4), pp. 190-7.

Whittington, C.J., Kendall, T., Fonagy, P., Cottrell, D., Cotgrove, A., & Boddington, E. 2004, 'Selective serotonin reuptake inhibitors in childhood depression: Systematic review of published versus unpublished data', *The Lancet,* vol. 363, pp. 1341-5.

Wodak, A. 1991, 'Is marijuana bad for you?', *Patient Management,* vol. 15(3), pp. 70-1.

AUTHORITIES AND INSTITUTES

Australian Institute of Health and Welfare, 2003, *Statistics on Drug Use in Australia 2002,* (Drug Statistics Series no.12), AIHW, Canberra.

Australian Institute of Health and Welfare, 2002, *2001 National Drug Strategy Household Survey: First Results,* (Drug Statistics Series no.9), AIHW, Canberra.

The United Nations Office on Drugs and Crime, 2004, *UNODC World Drug Report 2004,* United Nations, Vienna.

The United Nations Office on Drugs and Crime, 2003, *UNODC Ecstasy and Amphetamines Global Survey 2003,* United Nations, Vienna.

US Food and Drug Administration (FDA), Center for Drug Evaluation and Research website, Rockville Md., viewed December 2004, <http://www.fda.gov>.

United Nations, *Single Convention on Narcotic Drugs, 1961, as Amended by the 1972 Protocol Amending the Single Convention on Narcotic Drugs, 1961,* UNODC, Vienna, document viewed November, 2004, <http://www.unodc. org/unodc/index.html>.

United Nations, *Convention on Psychotropic Substances, 1971,* UNODC, Vienna, document viewed November, 2004, <http://www.unodc.org/unodc/index.html>.

LEGISLATION

Commonwealth of Australia, *Crimes (Traffic in Narcotic Drugs and Psychotropic Substances) Act 1990.*
Commonwealth of Australia, *Narcotic Drugs Act 1967.*

MEDIA/OTHER

Davidson, M.W. 2005, 'The endorphin collection' extract from Florida State University Research Unit website, Florida State University, viewed 21 January 2005, <http://www.micro.magnet.fsu.edu/index.htm>.
Friedman, D. 'Drugs and the brain', a lecture series for the US Department of Health and Human Services extracts from Friedman, D. 1990, *Focus on Drugs and the Brain,* Twenty-First Century Books, Frederick, Md.
WGBH, 1998, 'Role of Endorphins discovered', from the television program, *A Science Odyssey—100 Years of Discovery,* Public Broadcasting Service, Alexandria, Virginia, viewed 20 January, 2005, <http://www.pbs.org/wgbh/aso>.